WHAT THE DOCTORS ARE SAYING ABOUT

HOW TO RAISE A HUMAN BEING

By DR. LEE SALK and RITA KRAMER

"The authors are to be congratulated for providing a clear-cut, common-sense readable text on child development. This book clears the air of the large array of concepts in this field and substitutes simple guide lines . . . a volume of 'must reading'."—*Carl H. Smith, M.D. Emeritus Clinical Professor, University Medical College —The New York Hospital, and member of Editorial Board,* The Journal of Pediatrics

"The content is clear, succinctly presented, highly enlightening and sequentially informative . . ."—*Samuel Z. Levine. Former member of World Health Organization Expert Advisory Panel on Maternal and Child Health and President of the Society of Pediatric Research and American Pediatric Society*

"The first book for parents which stresses intellectual as well as emotional development, including material on the all important area of early stimulation, and bases what it says on research findings while avoiding technical jargons."—*Logan Wright, Ph.D. Director of Psychological Services, Children's Hospital, The University of Oklahoma Medical Center*

Also by Lee Salk

What Every Child Would Like
His Parents To Know

Published By
WARNER BOOKS

Lee Salk, Ph.D. and Rita Kramer

Director, Division of Pediatric Psychology,
The New York Hospital

Professor of Psychology and Pediatrics,
Cornell University Medical College

How to Raise a Human Being

A Parents' Guide

to Emotional Health

from Infancy

through

Adolescence

WARNER BOOKS

A Warner Communications Company

Library of Congress Catalog Card Number: 75-85593

ISBN 0-446-89479-6

This Warner Books Edition is published
by arrangement with Random House, Inc.

Cover design by John Harrington

Warner Books, Inc., 75 Rockefeller Plaza, New York, N.Y. 10019

A Warner Communications Company

Printed in the United States of America

Not associated with Warner Press, Inc. of Anderson, Indiana

First Printing: September, 1973

Reissued: August, 1977

10 9 8 7 6 5 4

To Eric and Pia, Debbie and Mimi

Contents

*How
to Raise
a Human
Being*

A Parents' Guide
to Emotional Health
from Infancy
through
Adolescence

LIFE WOULD BE a dull experience if it were true, as some people believe that the array of genes a child inherits from his parents determines irrevocably the kind of adult he will become. Fortunately, human development is more complex and more interesting than that, because absolute determination of traits by genes alone is a theoretical impossibility.

The biological, mental, and behavioral characteristics by which we know a person are the products, not only of his genetic constitution, but also of the physical and social forces to which he has been exposed. Genes constitute, so to speak, only latent potentialities which govern the mechanisms through which individuality is shaped by life experiences. It could even be said that man becomes *human* only through the stimuli he receives from society. All his distinctly human characteristics, such as speech, rational thinking, self-control, attitudes toward his fellow men, are acquired from the social group in which he develops. This is well demonstrated by the un-human behavior of feral children (children not raised among men) and by the great diversity of the mannerisms and ways of life that are peculiar to each society.

The responses that the person makes to environmental stimuli usually leave permanent imprints on him. This is especially true if the experience occurs early in life. Sigmund Freud emphasized that prenatal and early postnatal experiences condition mental attitudes and emotional responses even when the original experience itself seems to have been completely forgotten. Early experiences also affect profoundly many other attributes of the developing child—his biological constitution as well as his intellectual aptitudes. A scientific version of Marcel Proust's novel could be entitled *Biological Remembrance of Things Past*.

The imprints left by the child's experiences on his biological and mental individuality create a pattern on which all his responses to subsequent experiences are organized and become converted into structures, feelings, thoughts, and actions. This pattern thus imposes a direction that cannot be reversed on all biological and mental development. Hence, the tremendous importance for adult life of the child's early upbringing.

Laboratory experiences have provided striking illustrations of the fact that, in animals also, biological and behavioral characteristics can be conditioned irreversibly by influences experienced early in life. These experiments have yielded knowledge of the physiological mechanisms involved in conditioning and, more importantly perhaps, of the precise age at which animals can be conditioned.

The phrase "critical periods" denotes that in all animal species, and therefore probably in man, there are certain phases of prenatal and early postnatal life during which the characteristics of the organism are most susceptible to the shaping effects of surroundings, social influences, and other environmental factors. It is essential to use the phrase "critical periods" in the plural, because the various biological and mental characteristics do not develop at the same time and at the same rate. There may be one critical period for each one of the biological and mental characteristics.

The effects of early influences and their critical periods can of course be studied more conveniently in experimental animals than in human beings. Nevertheless, the knowledge of child development is extensive and profound, based as it is on the wisdom of the ages, now being supplemented by the scientific observations that have been made by pediatricians and psychologists during the past few decades.

Dr. Lee Salk and Rita Kramer present in this book a sophisticated distillation of both empirical experiences and scientific knowledge. They provide a practical guide for the understanding of children, and of their changing needs as their maturation proceeds through its various critical periods.

The affirmation that all aspects of biological, mental, and behavioral developments are profoundly conditioned by early influences, seems to imply a view of life as deterministic as the purely genetic theory. Yet, most of us believe that we can exercise a large degree of freedom in selecting our surroundings and formulating our courses of action, according to our own tastes and judgments. It seems useful, therefore, to conclude this preface with a few remarks on the place of determinism and free will in human life.

When the process of decision-making is analyzed in detail, all its components appear to be under the control of inherited genes, past experiences, and environmental forces. This appears to leave no place for real freedom of action. On the other hand, the awareness of freedom in making decisions is a straightforward experience, just as obvious and valid as the scientific evidence for determinism. Let me only state dogmatically that, surprising as it may seem, there is no real incompatibility between biological determinism and free will. The expressions of the genetic endowment that have been given shape by past experiences constitute the raw materials available to the person at the moment of decision, but it is free will that makes the decision. As shown by Dr. Salk and Rita Kramer, much can be done to provide children with the kind of influences that will enable them to develop their innate attributes and to express creatively their desire for freedom.

> René Dubos
> The Rockefeller University
> New York, N.Y.

April 7, 1969

Introduction: Helping You to Help Your Child

THIS BOOK IS BASED on the premise that it is easier to prevent emotional ills in infancy and early childhood than it is to treat them later on in life. Clinical observations of people and experimental studies of animals as well as humans have shown that early experiences have a profound effect on later behavior There are certain experiences which meet a baby's needs at different stages of his development in such a way as to encourage his growth. At the same time, it also appears that in the absence of certain conditions the infant or child may fail to thrive or to develop desired capacities for relating to other people or for learning.

These days, mothers and fathers are bombarded with advice, some of it spoken, some of it printed, and much of it contradictory. Parents have been increasingly pressured by commercial interests that capitalize on their desire to do the best for their children, from magazines that promise to reveal the answers to such questions as whether mothers should work or children should be spanked, to toy companies that warn you you'll never get him through first grade unless you use their products to program all his play activities every waking moment from birth on.

In the playground, at a dinner party, someone's always there to tell you what she thinks you should do about your baby's overdependence or his naps. Often it's hard to reconcile this advice with the last advice you were given on the subject.

All this is enough to make a nervous wreck of any conscientious parent in our increasingly competitive society.

Can anyone tell you how to be a good parent? Well, yes and no. No one can program parenthood for you day by day, and if they could it would take all the pleasure out of it anyway. We think most people have the innate capacity to be good parents. We believe good parents help their children develop the ability to cope with situations for themselves as well as the capacity to plan ahead, to be able to put off immediate gratification of their impulses for greater gratifications later on. This is the basis of the ability to learn and eventually to do one's life work, and the basis of the ability to love is the mutually satisfying attachment between child and parents from the beginning of life.

The question we've set out to answer for parents is this: What are the important principles you should apply in your own way to your own child? No two mothers or fathers are alike, and no two babies are born with the same constitutional endowment. So there can't be any exact rules for "managing" your child, any recipes for what to say or do in specific situations. Such a cookbook approach can't really help you; it only makes you feel inadequate when, sooner or later, you find you can't always do or say the specific thing recommended, and there you are, feeling miserable instead of enjoying your child.

You won't find any list of rules, any script to follow, any charts of ages and stages in this book. What you will find are general principles to be guided by in dealing with your own situation, your own life style, your baby's own personality, in order to meet his needs and help him grow.

Underlying the individual differences which make each human being unique, there is a general pattern of development that is the same for everyone. An understanding of this sequence of stages from birth to maturity, of what it is most important to have happen in each in preparation for the next, is the best guide for raising a healthy adult—together with a feeling for your particular child's characteristics.

In the early months of life the infant is helpless but capable of responding to many kinds of stimulation that will promote his mental and emotional growth. He is incapable of changing his own environment and depends on a mothering adult figure to meet his needs for various kinds of sensory stimulation just as he depends on her to provide the food that nourishes physical growth. The crucial thing in these early months of life is that all these needs be provided for in such a way that the infant establishes a positive and trusting relationship with the adult, that he comes to perceive human contact as rewarding.

Sometime in the second year of life, when the baby becomes capable of moving around on his own and interacting with more of his environment, the need is to set limits on his behavior and provide certain kinds of learning experiences by encouraging observation and stimulating awareness of his environment.

During the early school years the child begins to take his first tentative steps out of the home circle into friendships with other children and he learns to manipulate abstract symbols. In order to be capable of learning, he should already have developed both trust and self-control, the sense that it is worthwhile trying to please others and the ability to keep from acting on every impulse. This is the groundwork that makes it possible for him to acquire social behavior and intellectual skills, which in turn will help him through the essential process of his later school years, establishing his own identity as an individual.

In view of how children grow into adults, it is impossible to separate periods or processes. You won't find a separate chapter on the two-year-old, or one dealing only with feeding problems. We cannot talk about what a newborn needs without having in mind the needs of the child he will become, nor about how an adolescent meets the challenge of becoming independent without referring to the way his conflicts as a two-year-old were solved. And we cannot discuss feeding in infancy without also talking about crying, holding, sleeping, at the same age, because all are aspects of the same process, the way the infant comes to perceive and live in the world around him.

In focusing on human growth, describing the processes involved in the child's mental and emotional development, our purpose is to suggest certain kinds of experiences that serve not only to avoid some of the causes of emotional illness but also to provide for the greatest possible degree of healthy development for each child in terms of his own potential.

In a way, we'll be guiding you in using what you already know. You don't come to parenthood totally unprepared. Even if you've never held a baby or given one a bottle, never babysat or changed a diaper, you have the whole history of the human race behind you.

Human beings have evolved all the way from single-celled organisms by a process called natural selection, which has given us enormous built-in capacities to adapt "instinctively" to most situations we are likely to encounter, including, and perhaps especially those such as, child rearing. We feel that most of the time mothers have an intuitive feeling for the right thing to do, something that has been underplayed by child-care experts. Even the best specific rules for bringing up children are easily misunderstood and misapplied and in the end often serve only to discourage and depress mothers and alienate them from their own sense of motherhood. Most mothers have a basic tendency—unless it's distorted by culture or by emotional illness—to do the adaptive thing, the thing that will help a child survive and thrive.

You can see this tendency operating in any hospital maternity ward when a mother stands peering anxiously through the glass window of the nursery at her crying baby. She is obviously uncomfortable, and her anxiety is caused by her strong feeling that she wants to go to her baby, pick him up and hold him. She feels a need for him, just as he needs her to relieve his tensions. Nature has made her the baby's tension-regulator, the means of relieving his discomfort until he is ready and able to do so for himself. His signal—crying—and her response—comforting—are built in by nature.

We don't think anyone can tell you when to pick your baby up and when not to. What we think *can* be done is to acquaint you with what experimental research and clinical experience tell us, for example, about why babies cry, so that you can decide for yourself how to handle the matter.

Our goal is to help you use your natural tendencies as a parent, guided by the knowledge of what research has shown about the needs of the young infant—what strengthens the human being's capacity to deal with later

19

stresses. We hope to provide scientific information about the kinds of experiences to provide *in general* for different phases of development, what kinds of problems are likely to arise at certain stages and some useful ways of handling them.

As we look at what the evidence has shown about what's best for babies, you'll probably be able to find many situations where you know the "wrong" thing was done, and yet no discernibly dreadful results ensued. This doesn't disprove the evidence. For one thing, all scientific generalizations apply to statistical averages and need not fit a specific individual like a glove. Such generalizations represent *average* findings.

In addition to preventing disturbances, we are concerned with making the most of the possibilities for healthy growth and development. To say, for example, that the evidence suggests it's not a good idea to let babies in the first year of life "cry it out" is not to say that anyone who was allowed to cry much is bound to be disturbed as a result. What we are really saying is that there is a higher incidence of disturbance of certain aspects of personality among individuals who were left to cry for long periods of time in the first year of life than among those who were not. Of course you can find many individuals who were allowed to cry very early and are not in mental hospitals. But then, too, you don't know how much more happy or productive they might have been if their experience had been different!

A word about gender. It would be helpful if we had a word that meant both "he" and "she." Since English doesn't provide us with one, we'd rather go along with the usual practice of using the masculine pronoun, instead of referring to a baby as "it." We hope parents of girls will forgive us, and we assure the reader that unless we're talking about something where sex makes a difference—and we'll be careful to say when it does—everything we say about "him" refers to "her" as well.

PART 1

The Early Months
of Life:
From Birth to Mobility

1

The Nature of Mothering

MODERN SCIENCE has clearly established, both in animal work and in studies of humans, that early experiences have an impact on later behavior which in most instances sets a direction that is never reversed. Even though they are not remembered, these early experiences are generalized in many ways that affect later feelings, thoughts and actions. This has both positive and negative implications. On the one hand, the foundations of a healthy personality are laid from the first moments of life. And by the same token much of the serious psychopathology that occurs at a later age is directly related either to certain experiences or to the lack of certain others during critical periods early in life. Many of these personality aberrations, or psychotic conditions, are resistant to treatment.

The number of people in mental hospitals who respond to psychotherapy or other treatment is relatively small, and the staff in mental hospitals available to treat these people is pitifully inadequate. Even if we put every psychiatrist, psychologist and psychoanalyst in the country to work tomorrow treating the present population of our mental hospitals, they could hardly make a dent in the problem. And even if they were all to devote their time to training more professionals for the task at hand, it would take so long to do the job that most of those who are seriously mentally ill today would be past help before we had any means of reaching them.

It's a grim picture, and one which leads to the conclusion that we must focus on the problem of prevention.

Recent research on the development of the human infant provides striking evidence that early experiences can have great impact on the infant's emotional and intellectual growth. Therefore, it is our firm belief that we can strengthen the capacity of human beings to deal with later stresses by providing them with certain experiences very early in life.

The "baby watchers" in the research field tell us that within their first twenty-four hours infants are already capable of learning—that you can condition a newborn baby to a particular stimulus so as to get a predictable response. As a matter of fact, you can even condition the fetus before it is born—produce responses to external stimuli that the mother shows no conscious awareness of.

Newborn infants already have an impressive capacity to receive information from the environment through their senses—vision, hearing, taste, smell, touch, sense of movement. In any kind of learning—in any situation later on in life that requires receiving information from the environment which the individual processes and then utilizes—it is the sensory apparatus that provides the information for the various response mechanisms which we call behavior.

When babies develop and exercise their senses, they do not seem to be as easily overwhelmed by new and different experiences as babies who have not had much sensory stimulation. If you keep an infant in a clean, white, quiet room where there is very little of anything to look at or listen to or feel—very little change of any kind—for a long period of time, he will not have much chance to develop the ability to handle such stimulation later on. He needs practice in responding to stimulation—in looking at, listening to, and feeling different things, in order to develop the capacity to respond to more complex sights and sounds, to perceive different feelings and distinguish between them. We see this dramatically illustrated in animals which experimenters have isolated from any kind of sensory input during critical periods of time, keeping them in rooms where light and temperature remain constant and in which they see or hear nothing and are never touched or handled. When they are released, these animals respond amazingly like schizophrenic children. They do not make eye-to-eye contact or relate to others. Furthermore, they do not show the capacity to learn from experience later in life.

All this suggests that there are periods in development when we could present information—sensory input—to a baby which he could make use of later on. Even if he does not "understand" it, or integrate it in any meaningful way that we can observe at this time, we know that he adjusts himself to a higher level of stimulation—he can perceive a pattern of a certain degree of complexity or distinguish a particular sound—and that it requires much more stimulation later on to disorganize him. He learns to "recognize" the configuration of a human face or the sound of a voice, to perceive it separately from the confused mass of undistinguished sights and sounds around him. Let's consider what implications this has for the prevention of emotional disturbance.

We suggest that when a baby is taken care of by his own mother she has an attitude toward her child which nobody else really has. Of course, there are exceptions, but by and large nature has provided a system for the care

27

of the young which it would seem best not to interfere with. When we do, we sometimes find later that we were interfering with the development of some very important processes.

For instance, when lambs and goats are separated from their mothers immediately after birth and kept apart for even a short time—it may be no more than an hour—the mothers tend to reject them. They accept others just as readily as their own; in fact, they no longer seem to differentiate their own young and often fail to lick them, a very important kind of sensory stimulation for the newborn goat which also helps the mother to identify it. In some cases the young who do not experience this licking never stand up and even fail to survive. It seems that without the proper kind of maternal stimulation immediately following birth these young animals weaken to such an extent that they die off—and thus do not pass their genetic material on to another generation in the evolutionary process.

If we think about the human mother, who also seems to demonstrate certain tendencies toward her young almost automatically following birth—a desire to touch her baby, look at him and "talk" to him, hold him to her breast—we begin to wonder about the wisdom of our common practice of separating mothers from their babies immediately after delivery and keeping them apart for most of the next few days.

The mother-child attachment is crucial at this stage of development, and it may be that there are certain biologically determined tendencies a mother has following birth which do not develop if she does not experience the stimulus of her newborn baby's presence at that particular time. Are there responses which unfold under natural conditions but which in our culture we are inclined to interfere with too lightly?

A mother has a natural tendency to smile back at her smiling baby, and he learns from her delighted responses, which give him pleasure, to smile back at her again. Is there really any adequate substitute for a warm, responsive mother? Most of the time, to even the most conscientious nurse or maid, child care is a job, a "living." And to even the most responsible, it becames a daily routine. Is it realistic to expect that under these circumstances a baby will be offered an amount of stimulation comparable to that offered by his own mother when nothing interferes with her natural feelings of mingled joy and pride, wonder and worry, her sensitivity to his cries and her desire to hold and carry him?

There is nothing mystical about this. On the contrary, there seems to be good scientific evidence that every mother has a tendency toward these feelings after giving birth and that—by leading her to respond to her baby and to stimulate him in turn—they work to the mutual advantage of infant and parent in establishing a relationship in which the infant will thrive.

Parents sometimes take the attitude that caring for a newborn is a rather tedious job that one can always turn over to somebody else, or even that a nurse may do a better job because she is a "professional" and has had more experience. The professional baby nurse sometimes even takes a possessive attitude toward the baby and the parents begin to feel guilty about "interfering." But it's possible that in this situation it is really the nursemaid who is interfering between the mother and father and their newborn child; we may be interfering with a natural process when we separate parents from their infant too early in the child's life.

Then, too, a woman who is hired to take care of a child is sometimes unqualified to deal with the kinds of problems that arise. It is risky to turn an infant in this critical early period of life over to someone who is un-equipped to understand or respond to his real needs. He may learn patterns of behavior that cannot prove adaptive to your way of life. And he may find it difficult to learn certain kinds of behavior later on, having missed the pe-riods when he normally would have done so.

In the first weeks and months of life, the point is that the person who cares for the child, being more detached and "objective" than his mother, may by this very token lack her sensitivity to his cues and tend to care for him by preconceived rules and convenient schedules rather than by responding to his own signals of need and signs of comfort. The important thing becomes keeping him clean, or getting him to finish his bottle and go off to sleep "on time." Under these circumstances a baby may receive adequate physical care and yet miss out on the amount of stimulation—the holding, handling and cud-dling, the responsive faces, voices and hands—that give him an extra sense of pleasure in life beyond just being full and dry and that make other people seem worth re-lating to.

Later on, surrogate parents may interfere with a child's optimal development in other ways.

Children begin to learn social behavior sometime in the second year of life. They do this largely not through in-struction but by imitation. Leaving a young child with someone whose manners and ways are totally different from yours encourages the child to be like that person, no matter how often he may be told to be like you. And it only takes one visit to a park or playground to observe how many "advantaged" young children are disregarded by the very caretakers whose presence is presumably one of the advantages of their parents' affluence. They may not be in obvious distress or danger, but they very often seem to be capable of responding to more than they are being given in the way of stimulation.

On the other hand, if you are with your child most of the time you can teach him by the example of your own behavior in the natural course of things all the aspects of your own culture and background—manners, facial expressions, attitudes—which you value and which give you a sense of gratification in the child, which in turn gives him a sense of reward. If he has positive feelings toward his parents as the sources of pleasure and comfort, he won't need more reward for his behavior than pleasing them, which means being loved by them.

We don't mean to suggest that parents should never allow other people to look after their children. What we *are* suggesting is that parents choose these people carefully. Many people seem to give more thought to choosing a mechanic for their car than selecting someone to take care of their children. They will hire any able-bodied person to be with their children for hours at a time, day after day, as though it made no difference to the development of the child's capacities. But it does.

In addition to the effects of parents' own early experiences in determining their likes and dislikes, their habits and styles of behavior, there are often forces that affect their attitudes about themselves and their children. In addition to the personal dimension, there is the social one.

Every time you take your child to the park or the playground, you meet other parents. They watch your child and you; sometimes you find yourself talking with them. Before you know it, you're being invited to make some kind of comparison between their child and yours. (Does he sleep through the night? Eat by himself? Is he toilet trained? Can he read yet?)

If your child is around the age of two and you haven't done much about trying to toilet train him yet, if he's three and you haven't tried to teach him to read, it's hard not to feel put down when other parents boast of these accomplishments in children the same age as yours, even though up to now you may have felt there was no point in pressing toilet training for another half year or so and no good reason for pushing reading ahead of other skills at this age. You find yourself beginning to feel inadequate, wondering if you've botched up the whole business of parenthood already, and then trying to compensate somehow by treating your child differently.

Your child can really be the loser in such a situation. You may have been doing a better job of meeting his needs before you found out what your neighbor—or *her* neighbor—was up to with *her* child.

What we're suggesting is that as parents you have to come to terms with some of your own natural tendencies, your own desires, your own feelings of how best to bring up your own children, in spite of—sometimes even in the teeth of—social influences.

Some parents come from cultural groups in which "you have to have a nurse" to take care of the baby when you come home from the hospital. Not having one seems a reflection on your social status and many people think, Well, we can afford to have a nurse, having one seems to be the thing to do; it must be our shortcoming that having a nurse around makes us feel uncomfortable, so we'll have one whether we like it or not.

But something may cost a good deal and be in great demand and yet not always be in the best interests of your child. We might call this the "beriberi phenomenon." In the Orient, before the discovery of the effects of vitamins, only the rich could afford to eat polished rice, and so only the rich suffered from beriberi, which was caused by a deficiency of the vitamin B_1 that they were throwing away with the undesirable brown part of their rice.

Something like this often seems to be happening today in homes where children are raised by a competent custodial person who isn't much concerned with the emotional needs of children and whose job is primarily to keep them away from their parents except when the children are neat, clean and quiet. At other times the parents have little contact with the child and may never develop much of a real feeling for him. This situation can be disastrous for the child's emotional development. Who knows what goes on in that clean white room when the parents are not around? Often the child is being taught by the nurse not to cry, taught to do things in a clean, meticulous, rigid way. Even where this does not result in discernible damage, it may mean a kind of partial functioning in which the child never realizes his full potential.

Parents of "problem children" often say, "But we gave him the best of everything!" What they really mean is that they gave him the most *expensive* of everything—but not necessarily what would have been best to meet his particular needs.

Many people who have been brought up in well-regulated nurseries by maids or governesses grow up to be correct but cold, unable ever to feel much for other human beings. It's not that a baby can only form a strong reciprocal attachment with his natural mother. Millions of adoptive parents are proof to the contrary. It's just that there must be *some* kind of mutually satisfying relationship very early in life for healthy emotional development to proceed. And this is most likely to take place between a baby and his mother—or one who really *feels* like his mother, which in this case is the same thing.

Mothering, after all, is not just carrying a fetus and giving birth to a baby. It is continuing to care for that baby in a way which meets his needs while giving pleasure to both mother and child; and in most cases, if natural

33

processes are not interfered with, a woman's tendencies following pregnancy and parturition will lead to just that kind of care.

Let's turn from the various forces that affect people's attitudes about being parents and consider some of the kinds of natural tendencies that exist in the human being. Much of what we need to know about being parents we can learn from the animal kingdom. Granted that there is no justification for endowing animals with specifically human characteristics or for assuming that men must behave as rats or monkeys are observed to do in various situations, still it is equally unwise to ignore the evidence of general tendencies we observe in all animal species, of which we are one.

In most animals, we find a great need on the part of the parent to take care of its offspring when they are born; she will protect her young, even give up her own life for them if necessary. This is not "sacrifice." There is no reward for this kind of behavior. Animal children are never grateful—and once they leave home they never call up or bring the kids over on weekends.

It seems rather to be an instinct persisting through the evolutionary process, a tendency to behave in a way that serves to preserve the species.

Human mothers have such protective tendencies, too, although they are modified by culture and education. One such tendency we observe in the human mother is the need to have close physical contact with her baby, to hold and cuddle him. People have instincts and natural desires which have persisted through the whole development of mankind. Everything that has gone before in the evolutionary process is operating at any given moment in the here and now with a new mother. And it's possible that when you allow cultural influences to take over, allow other people to distort your healthy natural tendencies, you may be turning away from these things that are naturally appropriate to the development of healthy infants.

In trying to decide how to care for your baby—when to feed him, hold him, carry him around—if you sense a conflict between your own desires and the advice of friends, relatives or "experts" who don't know your baby, the best thing to do might be to ask yourself, "What does my baby really need at this stage of his development?" and "How do I really feel like doing this?"

This may prove a better guide than doing what will make somebody else think that you're a good mother.

2

Thinking About Development

HUMAN BEHAVIOR EVOLVES through a sequence of developmental processes. One way to look at this is as a series of critical challenges which all human beings experience. Exact ages vary, but the order is the same for everyone. How successfully each challenge is met is determined in part by how earlier challenges were met and in turn influences how the individual copes with later challenges. For instance, if an infant's earliest needs for food and comfort, contact and stimulation, are gratified in the stage of total dependency, he develops a sense of trust that becomes the basis for learning to move around on his own, away from his mother, at a later point in childhood.

The infant's needs must be satisfied in a way that fosters an interest in others outside himself. The toddler's investigation of the world beyond his own body has to be encouraged in a way that also teaches him to restrain many of his aggressive impulses. The child in school must learn to manipulate symbols and to solve social problems as well as intellectual ones and begin to practice the kind of independence he will have to establish in his teens. The adolescent has to cope with profound physical and emotional changes at the same time that he begins to free himself from his parents and find his own adult role.

Avoiding emotional disturbance and encouraging a child's fullest development depends on understanding what the essential goal of each developmental process is, and what general conditions will help him meet it so that he is ready to go on to the next stage. Cut-and-dried answers to questions like "Which is better—breast-feeding or bottle-feeding?" or "When should you wean a baby?" are a hit-and-miss affair at best. It's more helpful for parents to have an idea of the main goals to be accomplished in the period of an infant's total dependency and the meaning of feeding in that process, and use this as a basis for choosing specific methods which are consistent with developmental goals and which also "feel right" to the individual mothers and fathers who have to use these methods in their everyday lives.

Although they may not usually be grouped together, there are three men from different fields of science whose ideas converge in this view of human development. They are Charles Darwin, I. P. Pavlov and Sigmund Freud—a naturalist, a physiologist and the founder of psychoanalysis. Each of them was concerned with some aspect of the interaction between the organism and its environment—Darwin with the evolutionary development of mankind, Pavlov with the fundamentals of the learning process, and Freud with the effects of unremembered early experiences, which although forgotten, are not gone. Because so much of what we understand today about what children need and how parents can best meet their needs in the early years of life is based on work which has its roots in these ideas, a brief look at the general direction each of them gave to modern thought about the human organism and the human mind seems like a good place to start our discussion of how to prevent serious emotional disturbances in early childhood.

A century ago, Darwin traced the evolution of living organisms from simple to complex forms and showed that in the course of evolution each species has developed ways of adapting to its environment.

In order to survive, all living things must have the capacity to obtain from the environment certain things they need for existence. Animal behavior at every level from the simplest one-celled animal to man, the most complex of all, has to do with getting these needs met, with maintaining the organism in a state of equilibrium in which it can protect itself from danger, find food, and eventually reproduce. The apparatus which maintains this "steady state" and regulates behavior in the animal is the nervous system.

One way in which animals interact with their environment is through instinct or reflex behavior, an inborn pattern of response to certain situations. To take an example from the behavior of the human infant, when a baby feels hungry, he cries. He does so instinctively. No one has to teach him to cry.

Biologists from Darwin to the present time have compared the behaviors of different species along the evolutionary scale. They have found that the more complex the nervous system, the more flexibility a species has in adapting to its environment. The simpler the nervous system, the more dependent the animal is on instinctive or reflex behavior and the more bound to its special environment. If that environment changes so that it no longer meets the animal's needs in the same way, its behavior may become inadequate for survival. "The cornered amoeba cannot escape by flying."

One kind of learning in animals is called imprinting.

Studying the behavior of animals in their natural living

conditions, ethologists have observed in the young of a number of species of birds and animals what seems to be an inborn tendency to follow the most prominent moving object they encounter in the critical period following birth. This object is usually their mother. The process by which they learn to follow an object is called imprinting. If a young animal is kept from its mother during the time when it would normally be imprinting to her, it loses its capacity to develop this attachment behavior. With no strong bond established between them, the mother herself often ignores this infant and may even neglect to feed him. Instead of staying close beside her, he may wander aimlessly into dangers of one sort or another. He thus loses the opportunity to learn from his mother's behavior ways of dealing effectively with his natural environment. It's easy to see that his chances of surviving to adulthood are small compared with those of infants in whom nature has been allowed to take its course during the critical period after birth in which a strong reciprocal attachment between mother and newborn is formed.

There do not seem to be "critical periods" in as strict a sense at the human level of biological organization—periods which, once passed, can never be made up. Man certainly has greater flexibility in his capacity for response than those animals in whom instinct plays such a large part in the process. His highly developed brain and nervous system make him less dependent on instinct for his behavioral responses. He is able to learn from experience, to vary his response according to the conditions he meets in life, to a far greater degree than animals with simpler nervous systems.

In infancy we observe definite tendencies for the development of certain responses at certain ages and it seems clear that there are certain periods which afford the *best*

—if not the only—opportunities for the fullest development of one adaptive capacity or another.

It may be that one unique adaptive characteristic of human beings is the length of our critical periods. But even with this much greater degree of leeway than we find in lower animals, there are limits. For example, if a human infant does not form a strong reciprocal attachment to one mothering figure sometime during the first year of life, his capacity to form loving relationships with other human beings seems to be permanently impaired. Similarly, if no firm and consistent limits are set for a child's conduct by the time he goes to school, it is unlikely that he will ever be able to develop an adequate system of internalized controls.

By the time people grow up they learn various ways of getting fed when they are hungry. Depending on the circumstances in which they find themselves, they can go hunting or picking, buy something in a grocery store, go to a restaurant, or help themselves from the refrigerator. But for many months after they're born, all they can do to get themselves fed is cry. The ability to learn a greater repertoire of possible responses allows man to adapt to more varied environmental conditions than other animals, and even to alter the environment. But the more complex human nervous system takes a relatively long time to mature. It not only confers on man an increased capacity for adaptive learning, but a prolonged period of dependency as well.

Today, it is an accepted idea in biology that each individual repeats the history of the species, that "ontogeny recapitulates phylogeny." What this means is that from the moment of conception, when the egg is fertilized, and during its embryonic development, it passes through the previous stages of human evolution. In the earliest stages of prenatal development the human embryo closely resembles the anatomy of a fish or, later, a four-legged animal. At one stage it has gill slits, at another a tail. In the course of development, these features disappear, to be replaced by other structures.

Just as ontogeny recapitulates phylogeny in the anatomic development before birth, the human infant starts life with most of his behavior under reflex control and gradually replaces much instinctive with learned behavior.

Newborn babies all have certain natural tendencies, such as the rooting reflex, which helps them find the breast when they are hungry. In response to a touch near the mouth, they turn toward the side they were touched on and begin to suck. After a time they lose this rooting response and come to rely on learned behavior. They recognize the sound of their mother's voice, or the sight of a nipple.

Babies begin to lose many of these inborn neurological patterns of response as their nervous system matures and they learn other methods of responding. This is the rhythm of development.

Are there factors in the interaction between mother and child which are disregarded today but which have persisted through human evolution because they served an important adaptive function? We're inclined to think that we should do as little as possible to interfere with the integrity of the mother-child relationship during its early days. It may very well be that some modern practices interfere with the interaction between mother and child that is crucial to the development of a bond between them. There is reason to think that instead of separating mothers and babies after birth and keeping them on opposite sides of a glass window, the mother should be given her baby following delivery and allowed to keep him with her, hold him and take care of him.

We suspect that when parents can hold and nurse, pick up and cuddle and "talk" to their young babies they begin to realize themselves more fully as parents—to feel "motherly" and "fatherly." And we know how much early handling influences the behavior of the newborn baby himself. We find that when babies are given more stimulation —more handling, more to look at and listen to—they begin to develop a wider range of responses.

The human infant may be helpless, but he *is* responsive. Recent studies of perceptual development in infants show how much they see and hear. We are beginning to realize the extent of the interaction between the young infant and the environment, and the importance of providing conditions early in life which help develop certain capacities.

The human brain and nervous system is the basic apparatus, evolved through millions of years of nature's trial and error, that has the capacity to alter its own functioning in response to certain experiences during infancy. It starts out as a primarily biological apparatus, which regulates instinctive behavior, and develops, by the end of infancy, into the basis of a largely psychological apparatus, one which is capable of learning from its experience.

The patterns of behavior that develop earliest seem to be the most persistent, the most resistant to change. For example, nutritional habits acquired early in life persist or are imprinted in the organism. In a series of experiments, René Dubos was able to demonstrate this by showing that the first food animals were given after weaning became the one they preferred from then on when they were given a choice—whether it met their nutritional needs or not. And recent work by Czechoslovakian scientists suggests that even the biochemistry of body metabolism can be affected by early feeding experience.

It was Pavlov who demonstrated the capacity of an animal to learn from experience and associate one stimulus with another stimulus that happens to be present at the same time—what is called the conditioned response. In a classic series of experiments he rang a bell and at the same time presented a dog with a piece of meat. When presented with the meat, the dog salivated. After this procedure had been repeated a number of times, the sound of the bell alone caused the dog to salivate. There was no longer a need to produce the original stimulus, the food, in order to create the salivation. Pavlov had thus created a physiological response to a stimulus with which it had no functional relationship. This is learning by association, which is fundamentally different from the kind of behavior we described when we talked about imprinting, an inborn tendency to respond to certain stimuli. Conditioned responses are relatively easy to modify, whereas imprinted responses are not.

Learning theorists have found that if an animal is in a high state of arousal—in the grip of some strong feeling, physical or emotional—the strength of conditioning is much greater. In other words, if the animal is hungry he is more interested in the meat and more responsive to the bell as well.

In associative learning, there is always some reward. Either the learner is given something positive—some pleasure—or something negative—some pain—is taken away. In an imprinted response, no reward is necessary.

The individual may not be consciously aware of the second stimulus—the ringing bell—but he will still respond to it.

This brings us to Freud, who saw how the biological needs of infancy become the basis of psychological needs later on in life. He showed how early experiences exert an influence on later behavior: that although forgotten, they are not obliterated. Traces of every experience—even the very earliest—remain in the mind, together with ideas associated with them, and these associations persist into adult life, in the unconscious processes of the mind.

In one series of experiments that illustrate this point, a group of college students were presented with a series of words. One particular word—"cow"—was selected, and the subjects received a mild electric shock a few seconds after it had occurred. Instruments were used to measure their autonomic nervous system responses, such as heart rate and blood pressure, and it was found that afterward the subjects showed a definite response, indicated by such physiological signs as heart-rate changes, to rural words that suggest "cow"—words like "plow," "haystack" and "farmer."

Interestingly enough, when the subjects were asked afterward whether they remembered what word had preceded the shock, they could not identify it. They did not consciously connect the shock with the word "cow." Yet evidently conditioning had occurred in association with the stimulus word which, without awareness, they had learned to generalize to other words.

Such unconsciously formed reactions are common. Something that occurred in association with a painful early experience may continue to distress a person even after he has grown up and can no longer recall the original experience. For instance, a very young child subjected to a painful surgical procedure may seem to have forgotten all about it, but forty years later the sight of a white coat may upset him without his being able to say why he feels so uncomfortable.

Until fairly recently babies were thought to be almost like vegetables, perceiving little and hardly responding to their surroundings at all. Today we are finding that babies not only respond to sights and sounds from birth but actually begin to learn at the very start of life.

Essentially, an emotional disorder is a response that at

one time in early life was adaptive—served a useful purpose—but which has been carried into adulthood where it is no longer useful and prevents the individual from developing patterns of behavior that enable him to meet life's challenges in ways that do him—and society—the greatest good.

It was Freud who showed how early impulses are often reflected in adult behavior in the form of responses that are no longer useful to the individual.

For example, the strong attachment of a two-year-old to his parents helps him to learn by making him want to be like them. But unless he is able to loosen that attachment by the time he is five or six and divert his energies to learning at school and to forming relationships with other people outside the family, the persistence of that deep attachment into adult life can make it very difficult for him to function successfully in work or marriage.

Darwin's theory of the evolution of living things, Pavlov's demonstration of conditioned learning, and Freud's idea that early experiences persist in the unconscious mind and influence later behavior have led to a body of studies, experiments and observations that illuminate the process by which a baby grows into a healthy child and eventually a mature person.

All parents are bound to meet the needs of their children—as they do everything else—in somewhat different ways, since in each person there persist traces of his own early experiences and the intricacies of the connections made by conditioning and association.

The real job of parents is to stimulate patterns of behavior and personality that make as much as possible of the individual child's capacity to deal effectively with the environment into which he's born—to grow up able to love, to learn, to work, and eventually to be a good parent himself.

3

The Newborn:
What Is He Like?

WHAT AN INDIVIDUAL is like at any given time is a result of all the experiences he has had from the moment of birth —and even before. What this means is that to a great extent he is influenced by events he no longer remembers —what is called the unconscious processes of the mind.

Until about twenty years ago babies in the early weeks of life were considered to be relatively unresponsive to the world around them, incapable of learning from experience because of their undeveloped sensory apparatus. In the last two decades scientists have amassed an enormous body of descriptive literature, based on experiments and detailed observations, which shows that at—and perhaps even before—birth, human beings have striking capacities to receive sensory stimulation, engage in integrative functions and adapt to their early environment. Furthermore, it has been clearly established that early experiences have a marked influence on later behavior and that this behavior is harder to change than behavior resulting from later experiences. Not only can very early experiences contribute to disturbed behavior; they are also vitally important in the prevention of serious emotional disturbances.

Yet even today, many people still think you shouldn't pick a newborn baby up except when necessary to feed or change him. ("You'll spoil him.") They think he can't see. ("He can't focus. It's all just a big blur to him.") Or hear. ("His ears are still full of fluid.") That a three-week-old doesn't really smile ("It's just gas") and doesn't really know his mother ("He can't tell your face from a clock on the wall"). They think he should be kept in a quiet room as much of the time as possible ("All he really needs besides food is sleep"), and that since he is unaware of what's happening around him it makes no real difference what you do as long as he's fed and kept warm and dry. ("It doesn't matter whether his mother or a nursemaid takes care of him when you come home from the hospital.") And how often have you heard it said you should let the baby "cry it out"? ("He's got to find out who's boss. He has to learn he can't control you.")

These are accepted attitudes among numbers of intelligent well-educated people. Even professionals. Even—sometimes—doctors and nurses.

As we look at these commonly held notions and at the scientific work that has changed our thinking along these lines, we should consider not only what is important in a baby's experience, but why.

If we begin by asking what a newborn human is like, we have to answer, Which one? A glance through a nursery window in any maternity hospital will reveal how different babies are. Fat and thin, pale and red-faced, thrashing and placid—no two look exactly alike to any sensitive observer. So before we talk about what all babies have in common, let's consider what makes them all so different.

For one thing, newborns aren't really all the same age. We count age from birth, but actually the baby has already been developing for some nine months when he is born. Premature babies may miss out on whole months of prenatal growth, and even some "full term" babies are born a week or two before their due date, while others don't put in an appearance for as much as a week or two after they were expected. The baby lying in the bassinet next to yours in the hospital nursery, born on the same day, may thus be weeks older or younger than yours. These are great differences, and an "older" newborn is likely to be better developed, stronger, able to suck more vigorously, less easily upset by sudden noises.

Then too, each baby starts off with different inherited characteristics from each of his parents and their families before them.

Genetic factors influence not only structural features of the human being, such as height, the color of the hair or skin, and certain properties of the brain and nervous system, but probably predispose him to certain kinds of behavior as well.

The number of combinations possible in a human being's genetic make-up is staggering. When we also consider that the ultimate outcome of many physical as well as behavioral characteristics depends on the circumstances met with in the environment, and that these circumstances are never quite the same for any two people, it's easy to see why there is bound to be an infinite variety among individuals. This variety is an expression of the flexibility— the capacity to adapt to various environmental conditions —that has made man such a successful product of evolution. In human beings the broad lines of development are genetic "givens" laid down in the chromosomes, but the finer points are filled in by the individual in response to the conditions he meets following conception.

Some babies are markedly more active, more easily aroused, more irritable at birth, than others. And such predisposing factors often influence the way the baby is treated. Certain characteristics tend to elicit certain responses from others. A placid baby may be left alone for long periods of time, and lack of stimulation may reinforce a tendency to passivity. An irritable baby may seem like a nuisance, a disappointment to his mother because he is so different from the expectations she had of what her baby would be like, and she may handle him roughly, increasing his irritability.

In addition to hereditary factors, the newborn also has been affected by his mother's condition during pregnancy.

The idea of the nine months preceding birth as a time in which development proceeds only along predetermined lines, unaffected by the life around it, no longer fits the evidence. Not only is the fetus influenced by the mother's nutritional state, and not only can it be affected by certain viral infections and drugs, but an impressive number of studies show that a mother's state of mind, through related physiological manifestations—such as the hormonal changes that are associated with severe anxiety—can affect the fetus too.

These studies have shown that extreme fatigue and severe emotional stress increase the level of fetal activity, probably as a result of an increased production of adrenalin transmitted from mother to fetus through the placenta. These very active fetuses seem to use more energy and store less fat than inactive ones, and usually weigh less at birth. Follow-up studies of such active fetuses after birth are especially interesting. They show a tendency to be more sensitive than other babies, as well as to be more advanced in their motor development, perhaps as a result of the "practice" the fetus had in the use of its motor system before birth

Recent research shows that despite the insulation of the womb, some sensations do get through to the fetus. The unborn baby responds to loud noises with increased heart rate and movement. What is more, after hearing the same sound a number of times, the fetus—like the newborn—"gets used to it" and no longer responds with increased activity.

Another influence on the baby is the experience of birth itself—the length of labor, type of delivery and effects on his system of whatever drugs and medicines are used. Studies of the effects of anesthesia and medications given to mothers during delivery show that the baby is affected by them too. The more drugs are used and the closer to delivery time they are given, the less alert and attentive the baby is, not only immediately after birth but also for several days afterward, when one would assume the effects of maternal medications to have worn off. Babies seem to be not less but *more* sensitive during the birth process.

Given all these variables, it's easy to see that any description of the "normal" baby is that of a statistical average. No individual baby should be expected to resemble such a profile in all—or even very many—particulars.

All these factors—fetal age, genetic make-up, the mother's condition during pregnancy and the birth process itself—explain why, within moments after birth, infancy researchers find significant differences already existing among babies in all the ways that can be measured.

As a matter of fact, investigators—the "baby watchers" at work, often under the auspices of the National Institutes of Health, in public institutions and university medical centers—have found that the ways in which newborns vary are both consistent and stable. That is, a baby who is more easily irritated by sensations when he is a week old will probably also be more responsive later on. Normally, active babies do not change to quiet ones, or slow feeders to fast ones. Some of the ways babies differ *at birth* include how much they move around, how frequently they bring their hands to their mouths, how persistently they will follow an object moving across their field of vision or pay attention to a sound they hear, and how strongly they suck. One study in which sucking was measured and recorded on a graph indicates that every baby has a pattern of sucking—characterized by its rhythm and vigor—that is as distinctive as his fingerprints.

This business of sucking behavior is a good example of how inborn tendencies and environmental factors interact to influence the individual's development.

A baby whose sucking is fast and strong is easier for a mother to feed than one whose sucking is weak and slow, and a mother may be either worried or annoyed by a baby who takes a long time to feed and doesn't drain his bottle or nurse at the breast with vigor. She may become upset and tense in her handling of the baby or depressed because she feels inadequate as a mother In either case feeding time will be unpleasant for both of them. It's important for mothers to realize that babies differ widely in how much food they need and how long they take to get it, because a mother's attitude in the mealtime encounter does so much to determine a baby's feelings about the world and his reactions to it.

It is clear from a number of experiments that another way in which newborn babies vary is in what scientists refer to as the threshold for excitation. That is, babies differ in the amount of stimulation they can cope with without getting upset. This applies both to the sensations that come from inside themselves—hunger or fatigue, for instance—and from outside—for example, cold or loud noises. When a baby is hungry, he is experiencing feelings from within which he is powerless to do anything about for himself. His tension increases until these feelings are relieved, as they must be, by someone in the outside world.

How great his capacity is to tolerate tension is an individual matter, varying from baby to baby, and a mother can only judge when her baby needs to be fed, and how much, by paying attention to the cues he himself gives her.

Just as babies have different needs, studies show that even as newborns they respond differently to various methods of soothing. Sucking works best with some, rocking with others, and some babies, once they are aroused beyond a certain point and their crying has reached a particular pitch, are difficult to quiet in either way, while others respond well to both methods of soothing. Here we find another critical area in mother-infant interaction. A baby may respond best to a method of comforting that doesn't correspond to what his mother likes to do, or has been led to believe should be done. If she feels she's not a good mother because it is so hard for her to soothe him, they are in trouble. A mother's feeling that either she or her baby is inadequate will translate itself into the way she handles him and, again, affect the way he experiences the world, both now and in later life.

For the first few months of a baby's life crying is his only way of signaling his distress, the first "language" he has to communicate his need with, and the appropriate way for a mother to respond to it is to try to find out what's wrong and make him feel better. The only one who can tell a mother what he needs and how much is enough —enough food, sleep, movement, warmth or sights and sounds—for *him* is the baby himself. As a matter of fact, all his behavior is a kind of language at this age. He shows his level of tension in his activity as he moves from sleep to quiet wakefulness to fussiness to crying and then, when his need is met and his tension relieved—whether by being fed or changed or picked up and held—to drowsiness and sleep again. A mother who's in touch with her baby responds to his own pattern. When he is tense and highly aroused she soothes him, and when he is quiet and alert she plays with him, talks to him and shows him things. She does this because it gives both her and the baby pleasure, not because she has been told it is good for him, but as a matter of fact it is.

And this brings us from how all these babies behind the nursery window glass—some sleeping peacefully, some thrashing about and flailing their arms, some pale and some crimson, some looking bigger and older than others —are different as individuals, to our next consideration— what it is they all have in common.

All of them are highly responsive to stimulation of many kinds. They are interacting with their environment to a far greater degree than we used to think. In fact, newborns can see, hear, distinguish smells and tastes and respond to touch and movement. How do we know? A considerable amount of recent scientific research provides the evidence.

First of all, there is the research on visual activity. The most recent studies of infants show that on the very day they are born they look attentively at things and can distinguish forms, and that within the next couple of days they will fix their gaze on an object within their field of vision and follow it with their eyes if it is gradually moved.

Full-term babies delivered normally, and in whom the effects of anesthesia and medication given the mother have worn off, have periods of quiet wakefulness when their eyes are open and seem to focus. They are alert to both sights and sounds, and investigation has shown that an encounter with an "interesting" or novel sight can stimulate a baby to pay attention, can even keep a drowsy baby awake for as long as half an hour.

An infant this age can distinguish colors but he is more responsive to pattern (the arrangement of details) than to color or brightness. Newborns definitely distinguish patterns and will spend longer periods of time looking at more complex patterns (like a bull's-eye, or the outline of a human face) than they will at similar but simpler ones.

Why should a newborn, before he has had any visual experience to learn from, pay more attention to the outline of a facelike pattern than to a bright color? Some scientists think this represents a built-in advantage for the human species, an adaptive instinctive trait which has persisted through evolution. They point out that pattern— the configuration of details—doesn't change like outline or size or brightness or color, which change with point of view, distance or lighting. Thus, the most reliable means of identifying people under different circumstances is by facial pattern And the best way of judging their attitudes —whether they're pleased or displeased—is by the details of their facial expressions. We'll return to all this when we talk about smiling.

In general, seeking more complex patterns and increased amounts of stimulation for the newborn is a way of giving him experiences with sensations that later on help him to learn more complex things. If he is kept from experiencing the sensations his curiosity directs him to, he may have less success in forming concepts and ideas about people and the world later on.

When he is awake, the newborn baby has long spells of staring in one direction, but if some object like a pencil or a toy is moved into his field of vision he will move his head and follow it with his eyes. He is beginning to "reach" with his eyes; he will follow with his hands later.

The newborn not only sees and distinguishes patterns, he also hears sounds and even distinguishes differences in pitch. Just as a baby a day old can follow a moving object with his eyes, he turns his head toward the source of a sound. He will often stop moving at the sound of a bell, as though "staring" at the sound. He feels changes in temperature, especially around his mouth; he distinguishes tastes, and is already beginning to prefer sweet ones. He is even beginning to distinguish smells, and he is very sensitive to touch and pressure.

In fact, a growing body of research reveals that the newborn baby is a far more complex, responsive, active creature than we used to think. It has also shown that the amount and kind of stimulation given to infants—from the earliest days of life—has a profound influence on the course of later development.

Studies of infants in institutions show that babies deprived of things to look at and touch, faces and voices to respond to, opportunities to move around, fail to develop the capacities on which later abilities depend. They become retarded, often irreparably so. Other studies have demonstrated that babies in settings that provide a good deal of such stimulation thrive in the early months of life.

These studies suggest that environmental conditions can affect basic bodily functions as well as behavior, that early sensory experience affects the nervous and endocrine systems, metabolic functioning, and other basic body processses. Thus those experiences may determine the kind of equipment the individual will have for dealing with the various stresses he'll encounter in learning to act and to think

What implications does this have for raising human beings? It is not always possible to predict the stresses our children will meet in the course of their lives so as to prepare them directly for these particular events. But as parents we *can* help them develop the strength and flexibility —a feeling of inner security, the ability to form warm relationships with other human beings, and the capacity to deal with increased stimulation or stress when it becomes necessary—that are the foundations of later mental health.

It's important to begin at birth, in the way in which one cares for a baby, responds to him, and provides him with nourishment, both physical and mental. In order to understand what this means in terms of daily life, which at first is largely a matter of eating and sleeping, crying and cuddling, let's take a closer look at the needs of this most complex, most adaptable—and most helpless—kind of infant, the human newborn.

Like all living organisms, the human infant must maintain an internal equilibrium in order to function. If he is to survive and develop, he must stay in a kind of steady state, not bombarded by too many unpleasant sensations from within his own body or overwhelmed by too much excitation from the outer world. Nature has arranged it so that the relatively helpless human infant has a special system for maintaining him in this "comfort zone," protecting him from either too much or too little internal and external stimulation. This system is his interaction with his mother. A mother serves as a kind of tension-regulator for her infant, providing him with what he needs. And who tells her what this is? In the beginning at least, he does.

An infant's crying seem to be a "signal device" to which his mother responds intuitively with comforting behavior. It is the natural thing for a hungry or cold, wet or tired, baby to cry, and the natural thing is for his mother to go to him, pick him up and hold him, feed him, keep him warm and dry, and rock him to sleep.

Although he seems to spend most of his time sleeping, the newborn baby is actually busy every moment adjusting to life "on the outside." His system is in a delicate state of equilibrium; he reacts with his whole body to sudden changes in temperature, touch, light and sound. He is powerless at this stage to control his sensitive reactions to the many little changes in the atmosphere around him. His periods of wakefulness range from a drowsiness that looks like a drugged stupor, usually just before falling asleep, to the wild flailing of arms and legs that accompanies his most frantic crying, usually just before feeding. In between, he has short periods of alert attentiveness. What he's like—and what he's capable of responding to at any given time—depends on his level of arousal at that moment.

We have seen that infants differ not only in their needs but also in their sensory apparatus. Just as some babies are more excitable than others, some babies are harder to soothe than others. Not all babies are quieted by the same things. Some prefer sucking, others prefer rocking, warmth or sound.

Babies in a hospital nursery where a tape recording of a human heartbeat was played have been found to cry less, gain more weight, show less restlessness and sleep better than others, perhaps because they are familiar with the pulsing sound that they had experienced in the mother's body before birth.

Most newborns are soothed by continuing low-frequency tones. This will come as no news to mothers, who are well aware of the soothing effects of music, the hum of motors, and the human voice in calming irritable babies, who usually stop their crying and thrashing about to listen. But sounds can also be exciting to babies who are in a quiet state. The same form of stimulation can be soothing or exciting, depending upon how aroused the baby is and how long it lasts.

A baby cries when he feels discomfort or pain because of some needs he has. In addition to their needs for food and sleep, babies seem to need a certain amount of sucking, even after they have had enough to eat; and in addition to being kept warm and dry, they seem to need a certain amount of contact and postural stimulation. Crying is the only way the baby has of letting you know when he needs relief. It's also his first form of social communication, because it calls forth a response from another person. Even scientists engaged in studying newborn babies admit they find it hard to observe a crying baby without getting up and doing something to relieve the baby's discomfort.

Babies have been found to cry more when they get less care and handling, even if they are well fed and changed whenever they need to be. Studies show that crying for "unknown causes" decreases sharply when babies get more mothering—more handling, more talking to, more chance to look and listen. Babies also seem to cry less if they are held close to their mothers' bodies.

The innately gratifying nature of physical contact between mothers and infants was demonstrated by Harry F. Harlow in a series of ingenious experiments with newborn monkeys in which some were fed from a bottle attached to a "mother" figure made of wire mesh, and others by one covered with terry cloth. All the monkey babies, regardless of which figure had fed them, chose to go to the terry-cloth mother and spend time clinging to her. When they were frightened, they ran to the terry-cloth mother, and when they were near her they were more adventurous about exploring the strange and the new. It seems that the stimulation provided by physical contact with a parent figure is rewarding in its own right and leads to an emotional attachment. But just as there is more to mothering than providing a baby with food, there also seems to be more to it than giving tactile comfort. The terry-cloth mother didn't do very well by her children in the long run. They grew up unpleasantly aggressive, were unable to make friends, and had sexual problems. These unhappy monkeys had gotten plenty of food and contact with a soft and warm inanimate surface, but received none of

59

the active, give-and-take interaction between mother and child that seems to be necessary for healthy emotional development.

The establishment of a bond between mother and child seems to require more than ministering to his physical needs for food and warmth, for relief from pain. Babies seem to have a need for a certain amount of stimulation as well—for what might be called play. This means various kinds of interactions between the baby and his environment in that period of quiet alertness when he is most capable of responding to the outside world.

Let's see what happens when infants receive this kind of stimulation and when they are deprived of it.

4

The Newborn:
What Does He Need?

RESEARCHERS CANNOT SET UP experimental situations to test their more radical theories on real children, but life sometimes does it for them. Some years ago, when psychiatrists and psychologists began to take a close look at infants whom private misfortune had consigned to public care, they were struck by the dramatic effects of sensory deprivation. Severe retardation was found to be common among infants who were kept in cribs with covered sides, given no toys, and had nothing to look at but a blank ceiling. These babies were fed, bathed and changed, but there was little for them to hear on the quiet wards, and they received little handling beyond routine nursing care.

In films made on hospital and foundling-home wards, even children in "good" institutions look out of dull, expressionless eyes, turn their heads away from the approaches of friendly adults, lie supine and quiet, their only game an occasional bit of play with their own fingers. One such little girl looks and behaves like a normal baby of about a year. She is almost two.

What is missing?

The complex interactions between mother and child that take place under normal home conditions provide satisfaction of his bodily needs, stimulation of his developing senses, and learning opportunities for both perceptual and motor skills and social behaviors. The response he gets from his mother and from the objects he acts upon encourages the child to continue acting. The child who consistently gets no response eventually gives up, becomes apathetic and indifferent to people. On the other hand, a child who has experienced other people as sources of pleasure continues to seek contact with others as he grows up.

Experiments in which animal mothers are separated from their young in the crucial hours following birth result in many cases in failure to establish the mutual attachment on which the development—and in some cases the very survival—of the young lamb or goat depends.

Is it valid to apply animal data to human beings? Comparative studies and observations by ethologists and anthropologists, experimental psychologists and clinicians, suggest that it would be foolish to ignore the obvious similarities of animal responses to human responses under certain conditions. When newborn human infants are deprived of sensory stimulation by a maternal figure they demonstrate behavior that is incredibly similar to the behavior of animals experimentally raised in a state of sensory deprivation early in life. Both the baby raised from birth in an institution and the monkey isolated from birth in a cage have severe problems in relating to others of their species. Neither of them responds appropriately to stimulation. Neither can learn much by experience. And after a while very little can be done to change either of them.

A knowledge of biological process and clinical observations both suggest that the mother-infant relationship in humans might be strongly influenced by the degree of contact and the kind of environment in which the mother and child are exposed to each other immediately after delivery. This may be particularly significant in the case of infants predisposed by constitutional factors to the severe and almost untreatable condition of childhood psychosis. Psychotic children are often unable to respond to any emotional or intellectual approach that is made to them. They do not make eye-to-eye contact with others, become increasingly irritable when approached, and are unable to form emotional attachments to other human beings.

One theory holds that a child may be predisposed to severe emotional disturbance owing to some weakness in his response mechanism and a deficiency of conceptual, motor or sensory apparatus, and that when this condition is aggravated by a mother's absence, neglect or failure to "get through" to the child, the result is psychosis.

A baby cries when he wants to be taken up and fed. His mother comes, picks him up, holds him and feeds him. He begins to associate these experiences with her presence. And eventually, the focus of his satisfaction shifts from his own body to the mother who does things that give him pleasure. A psychotic child never reaches this point in development. The child's focus of satisfaction is not released from within himself and he has little or no motive for responding to anyone else.

Severely disturbed children frequently have histories of being quiet, amenable and passive, and parents who thought of them as "good" babies because they were "no trouble." They could be left alone for hours at a time. Locked within themselves, they pursued their solitary rituals. Having failed to develop in infancy, the capacity to respond to other human beings seems to be lost to these children.

There is no way of knowing for sure whether greater stimulation and more responsive handling by warm parents would have prevented any particular case of severe emotional disturbance from developing, but an overwhelming number of psychotic children prove on investigation to have had—in addition to any predisposing factors—unresponsive parents who left them to cry for hours, their cries ending not with someone coming to ease them but with their own final exhaustion.

Under natural conditions, most mothers respond to their babies in ways which offer newborns the early sensory stimulation that helps develop their perceptual and response mechanisms and adapt to more complex patterns of stimulation. They talk to their babies and sing to them. They hang mobiles from the ceiling, tack pictures on the walls, put toys in the crib. There may be patterned curtains on the windows, painted furniture in the room. They vary what the babies see and are exposed to by carrying them from place to place. They rock them in cradles or rocking chairs. In all these ways they vary the environment while the child is still too young to do it for himself. Infants who receive this early stimulation—who are held, rocked, carried, talked to and smiled at—are less irritable, have longer periods of concentration, develop a wider range of different responses and relate better to other people. The more they see, hear and feel, the more they taste and smell, the more they get used to and the more they seek different experiences. In this way, early stimulation seems to foster greater learning. If the newborn infant is deprived of this early sensory stimulation, he may lose his capacity to develop certain adaptive responses to the world—such as taking an interest in people and objects outside himself—and show the persistent behavior and impaired functioning that are characteristic of childhood schizophrenia.

Evidence of the effects of early stimulation on later behavior comes from many different kinds of clinical and experimental work.

When laboratory animals are reared from birth in stimulus-deprived environments, in dark cages where they have nothing to look at, hear no sounds, and experience no touching or handling, they react in bizarre ways—with a startling similarity to schizophrenic children—upon emerging and encountering increased stimulation. If the stimulation of animals raised under natural conditions is increased, they react normally. Many investigators think it likely that the early deprivation of experience permanently affects the nervous system, endocrine system and muscles. It is through use, for instance, that the millions of new connections are formed between the millions of nerve cells throughout the animal's body, connections it will need later on to cope with increased amounts of stimulation.

Experimental psychologists working with animals report the finding of chemical and anatomical differences in the brains of rats raised in a stimulating environment as compared with those from the same litter raised in isolation. This seems to indicate that a genetic advantage can be lost if the environment doesn't encourage its development.

Previously lethargic babies in an orphanage, when given extra handling by the nursing staff, showed much greater eye-hand coordination at six months of age than those who received routine care. The babies who were given the extra handling also cried more when left alone, unlike the others, probably because they were beginning to form human attachments. They were also providing evidence for the idea that early stimulation, through activation of the perceptual apparatus, creates a need for greater stimulation, which might show up later as superior learning ability.

Babies cry when they have some need, or hunger, they cannot meet for themselves. The need may be for food or it may be for stimulation. There are experiments showing that babies not only stop crying when they are held and rocked, but also that such handling delays the onset of their crying and at times prevents it altogether.

Parents often find that when a baby is fussy and can't seem to relax and it's not clear what he wants, he may not stop crying when they pick him up and hold him, but when they start to walk with him he quiets down and is soothed. What they are doing is not only changing his position but lifting his head up, moving him around and giving him a chance to see different things. They are giving him what is called a kinesthetic sensation. His muscles and the apparatus that controls balance—the middle ear—are stimulated when the baby is moved around. The need for movement is one we all have. But babies are powerless to get up and move around by themselves at first. That's why the old-fashioned cradle and rocking chair have such universal appeal.

When babies receive a certain amount of stimulation, they accommodate or habituate to that level and seem to want more. Sometimes you'll find when a baby cries, he's just used to seeing what he's been looking at and can be satisfied by being picked up and carried around. You're changing the scene for him, and giving him feelings of pleasure in being moved around. Being picked up means to a baby that someone is providing him with some kind of sensory stimulation. It doesn't mean he's trying to run your life. He isn't even capable of such a conception. If parents pick a crying baby up, they needn't be afraid they are teaching him to control them. They are teaching him that something out there responds to the need he feels within, whether it is the need for physical sensation or for food. This is the important thing for babies to learn in the first months of life—that the world beyond the boundaries of their own bodies is a caring one, that there is someone who responds to their need to be free of discomforting tensions and that it's worthwhile reaching out to others. This attitude, learned in the earliest months of life, enables you later on to teach your baby skills and disciplines, set tasks and limits.

What scientists have been demonstrating is that from the time a baby draws his first breath—perhaps even before that—he is learning. At first, in the early reflex stage of his development, he learns through practice in coordinating his simple motor actions with what his senses tell him about the outside world. The more opportunities he is given to look, to listen, to suck, to touch different kinds of things, the more he learns.

A fussy baby usually quiets when given things to look at or to listen to. Unless he is hungry, he will usually have longer quiet periods and cry less if he is given toys in his crib or held up where he can see what's going on. The more stimulation he has a chance to get used to, the less easily he is upset by new sights, sounds and feelings. And developing the important ability to pay attention doesn't just come with age but depends on experience too.

A baby is most able to respond to novel sights and sounds when he is awake and comfortable, after he has been fed, diapered and burped. This is his natural play time, and for the early years of his life play and learning are inseparable. If an infant has to use all his energy to cope with strong feelings of distress from within, he can't pay attention to what's going on outside him. Research on the human infant shows that new-borns have the ability to focus their attention on a particular new thing they see or hear, that doing so quiets them and screens out distracting sensations, and that as a baby explores his environment he increases the number of things which interest him. "The more a baby sees, the more he wants to see." He is building a vocabulary of sense experience, so to speak, and forming abilities on which later learning depends: paying attention and developing specific controlled sequences of actions.

For example, practice in looking at things and in touching things enables him to differentiate these activities from the rest of his behavior and then relate them to each other in useful ways. First he has to learn to do these things separately. Then later he can purposely combine the acts of looking and touching until eventually he can reach out and take hold of something he sees.

What this means to parents is that in addition to babies' needs for food and love, they need other kinds of nourishment too. They need stimulation to grow on just as much as they need vitamins and minerals, warmth and tenderness.

The baby's "fussing" may be a signal provided by nature to make sure that he gets enough of the kind of stimulation that will be useful for his later intellectual development.

It makes no more sense to say of the crying baby, "He just wants attention," than it does to say, "He just wants food." Both are real needs. Don't let him "cry it out." Feed him if he's hungry, and if he's bored, change his environment for him. Pick him up and bring him into the family circle, where he can enjoy the feeling of being held and the many new sights and sounds he'll encounter.

Parents sometimes wonder if they can "spoil" a baby with too much cuddling. It's hard to see how a very young baby can have "too much" cuddling. With an older child, cuddling and holding him may prevent him from getting up and walking away from you when he's ready to pick himself up and get around. But in the early months of life, this hardly applies.

This is the time the child needs handling, holding and being carried around, because this is the time when he can't get up and move around by himself. He needs you to offer him stimulation. What you're doing in providing this kind of contact is helping to exercise his perceptual apparatus. You're exercising his sense of touch and movement, giving him visual experience, stimulating him to make sounds, to "talk" to you.

In many ways, you're teaching him to respond appropriately. When you smile at him, he smiles back at you. What you're really doing is giving him the raw materials he needs for dealing with later problems. If you continue this kind of stimulation and meet all of his physical and emotional needs now, when your child is able to get up and walk around he will want his independence. He will have a natural tendency to be autonomous, to do things for himself.

If, on the other hand, you decide to teach him to be independent now, by not responding to his cries, he may cling to you for a much longer time than if you had offered him gratification.

Just as you don't teach a child to be a football player by giving him a football at the age of three months, you don't teach him to be independent at three months or at six months by not responding to him. All he would learn is to detach himself from people and not rely on them to meet his needs.

Babies in institutions like hospitals and orphanages, where they receive little handling or stimulation, often don't look people in the eye. Even when someone picks them up and tries to get their attention, they don't look into the person's face. This failure to establish visual contact is one of the signs of emotional disturbance in babies.

Newborns have a natural tendency to look at moving objects, and a mother's face is usually the main object that moves in and out of their field of vision at first. It is a common impression that babies don't smile until they're about three months old, but smiling can be observed within the first month of life. This may be a rudimentary biological response, which later becomes associated with fulfillment and satisfaction, and then becomes a general response to many other kinds of pleasures.

Sometime around his fourth week, a baby will begin to smile. You may see the corners of his mouth draw up before this age, but he doesn't seem to be looking at anything in particular. In fact, he is usually drifting off to sleep at the time. But now, toward the end of his first month, he begins to smile at the sound of his mother's voice, probably because he has come to associate it with food and comfort. Now he looks you in the eye when you bend over to speak to him and for the first time you feel he is smiling at *you*.

What were those earlier grimaces? Well, it depends on whom you ask. Aunt Minnie would say "gas." A scientist would say "reflex." Twitching around the mouth is only one of the many involuntary little movements by which a newborn discharges tension as he relaxes and falls asleep. It also seems to be a reflex response to a mildly surprising event, just as an intense surprise evokes a startle. It takes on emotional meaning only as it becomes a means of social interchange between mother and baby.

We have already noted that infants in the first week of life can discern patterns and "prefer"—meaning simply that they spend more time looking at—a human face to other patterns. Babies seem to have a tendency to perceive the human face as potentially rewarding.

A baby smiles in mild surprise as he perceives a human face come into view. As mother bends over his crib, smiling and cooing while ministering to his needs, she reinforces his response, and smiling becomes associated with pleasure. Doctors have found that when the smiling that all babies show at this age meets with no response, as is sometimes the case with infants in institutions, they give it up. The baby's tendency to look at a human face may be nature's way of getting a baby to explore his own environment and establish a contact with his own mother.

When a baby is held and fed, he usually fixes his attention on his mother's face. His eyes open, and he becomes more alert.

It's possible that smiling may begin as an adaptive reflex, a relaxation of the muscles at the sides of the mouth when the baby is satiated and stops sucking. It may be a kind of tension-reduction response which, by introducing air at the sides of the mouth, causes the baby to release the nipple. Smiling then becomes a response associated with pleasure in general as the satisfied baby's smile is reinforced by his environment. It delights his mother and causes her to make sounds and touches that give him further pleasure; you might say the environment smiles back. In this way, the baby learns to connect the act of smiling with pleasure. Eventually, he smiles in response to many kinds of satisfaction.

Since for the first few months of life his mother is the major influence in a child's world, providing him with a stimulus-rich environment does not mean going out and buying a lot of expensive or complicated equipment. His needs for sights and sounds, touch and movement, are met by your face and voice as you bend over him to feed or bathe him, change and dress him, talk and sing to him, play with him and carry him around. Toys are fine, but mainly as supplements to the pleasures he experiences with you. They can be extensions of a mother's presence but they can't substitute for her absence, whether physical or emotional.

Movement is important—picking him up, walking with him. Color is stimulating too. Why should a nursery be pure-white and sterile looking? And there's no need to accustom a baby to going to sleep only in a quiet room. As a matter of fact, it may not even be a good idea to go tiptoeing around whenever he's asleep. The babies who can sleep through noise seem to be those who have been exposed to a lot of sound. If you accustom them to noise early enough, they begin to adjust to it; they adapt to it and can take much more, while the baby who startles at every little sound is usually one whose initial tendencies have been reinforced by being kept in a very quiet room. It has become increasingly clear that the amount of stimulation children adjust to early in life can be a significant advantage to them later on.

We know that babies who are picked up and moved around and given a great deal of visual stimulation develop better eye-hand coordination. Visual-motor coordination is crucial to later learning, particularly in learning to read and write, and children who are neglected in infancy are often retarded in the development of the integrative functions of the brain.

An infant may learn at a very early age, if no one comes to help him when he cries, that he has only himself to rely on. He learns to satisfy himself with whatever primitive means he has for handling anxiety—such as fantasy. In the cases of severely disturbed children, they may come to find most of their satisfaction through the fantasy world they have created. When this becomes more gratifying than the real world, they may never come back to reality.

There's no harm in a child crying; the harm is done only if his cries aren't answered.

Babies who are left to cry for long periods of time and

are overwhelmed by frustration develop neurotic behavior, in extreme cases even become psychotic. If you ignore a baby's signal for help, you don't teach him independence. How can a helpless infant be independent? What you teach him is that no other human being will take care of his needs.

Eventually, this can result in severe problems in a child's capacity to relate to other people. Of course, not every child who has been left to cry it out will grow up to be psychotic, but many of those who do show early signs of disturbance are children whose cries have not been answered. Eventually, they stop crying. They become very "good" babies who don't bother anyone. Actually, it's not that they've learned to be good, it's that they've given up. What they have learned is that there's nobody out there who answers their cries—so they might as well forget it. They've closed out the world and stopped relating to it.

You can teach a baby to give up eventually by not meeting any of his needs—by overwhelming him with frustration so that he turns into himself and his own rudimentary resources for gratification.

The work of the past three decades has shown that children raised in institutions under excellent sanitary conditions but left alone for long periods of time, where nobody picks them up and gives them adequate sensory stimulation, show signs of retardation in responsiveness as well as in motor activity and coordination. Furthermore, they don't learn to differentiate one person from another—or sometimes even to differentiate people from things. They have stopped reaching out to the environment to get a response, turned off their tendency to relate to other people.

No one knows for sure just how this happens, just what combination of biological and environmental conditions is at work in these children; but it seems that, given a certain predisposition—some constitutional vulnerability—children who are raised in an environment that does not provide certain kinds of experiences, that fails to stimulate certain kinds of physiological responses, eventually are affected by structural changes in their response mechanisms and later exhibit severely disturbed behavior.

What we have learned is not only that infants are highly responsive but that they need to be given things to respond *to*. We've discovered that if a baby is given a certain amount of stimulation—faces and voices, handling and motion, tastes and smells—he attends to these stimuli, he masters them, and then he begins to fuss because he wants to be given more novelty and adventure. He wants to master more new things. He's not "just fussing for attention." He really wants to experience more sights and sounds, and the more kinds of stimulation he masters now, the more he will be able to deal with later. This early stimulation not only fosters the growth of intellectual curiosity but strengthens his capacity to deal with transitions, his ability to face uncertainty and deal with new and unpredictable situations that will arise later in life.

An environment that provides enough stimulation helps infants learn to deal with greater stress. The baby who doesn't have enough varied sensory experience is easily overwhelmed. He may constrict his responses to the outside world and may even develop serious behavior pathology.

It would seem to be a good principle to follow, in the light of what we know about infant development, to try to make babies very happy in the first year of life, to minimize the amount of frustration they experience while they are totally passive and dependent.

Think of those early months. The baby is on his back or stomach, helpless. He can't move from one place to another or do anything for himself. The environment has to come to him.

If you meet the needs he has then, these needs disappear, to be replaced by others. The child will want to learn to walk, to explore his surroundings, to try new things. But if his early needs have been frustrated, he retains them, clinging to a wish for these early kinds of infantile gratification. He will want to go on being held and carried around.

However, a word of caution on this point: The principle involved here is to respond to the baby's needs as he communicates them to you—not to try to anticipate them. There are some mothers who seem to be standing there beside the crib all the time waiting for the baby to wake up, and just as soon as he opens his eyes they stick a nipple in his mouth because they don't want him to experience any frustrations. This is not what we're suggesting.

There has to be a certain amount of frustration in order for the infant to be able to associate the actions of the outside world with the gratification of his internal needs.

Through most of the first year of life the baby does not differentiate between himself and the world around him, between his actions and the results they may have on the environment. There is no "I" or "me" yet. The whole world is hungry, or warm, or wet, or painful, or feels good. During his first year he gradually begins to realize that there is an outside world of objects separate from himself and—most important—that he can produce effects on them.

If a mother gratifies an infant's every wish before he has uttered a cry, it is almost as though she is tuned in to his own body, as though whatever happens inside him she feels too. He may fail to make the distinction between "me" and "other," between himself and the outside world.

There should be some communication of need and then, before too long, some gratification should take place, so the child learns that if he asks for help, someone will answer.

5

The Feeding Relationship

A GREAT DEAL OF THE INTERACTION that takes place between mother and child in the early months of life centers around the feeding process.

Most parents are familiar with the breast-or-bottle controversy, and one of the first decisions a mother makes when her baby is born—if she has not made it even before then—is whether to nurse him or feed him a prepared formula.

Pediatricians familiar with metabolic functioning tell us that the human mother's milk remains unsurpassed as a food for the human newborn in its balance of the various nutrients important for growth and in the body's capacity to utilize these nutrients properly. In addition, breast feeding gives the most opportunity for contact between mother and child. It gives the baby the security of being held and supported as well as the tactile stimulation —the holding and touching—he seems to need.

Thus there are very good reasons for choosing breast feeding, both for its nutritional value and the opportunity it affords for close contact between mother and infant;

but this doesn't mean a mother should feel like a bad mother for not breast feeding her baby when she has overriding reasons of her own. It may be the ideal food, and the ideal feeding method, but a baby who is not breast fed need not suffer physical or emotional deprivation as a result, as long as he is given an adequate milk substitute recommended by a pediatrician, and as long as he is held, talked to and played with at feeding time.

The only way of feeding a young baby that is generally frowned on is propping his bottle in his crib or carriage and leaving him to drink it without being held. Even then, observers have noted that in some large families where a mother's many duties sometimes make bottle-propping unavoidable, babies have been known to suffer no ills as a result if they are given the propped bottle someplace where they are exposed to the sights and sounds of family life—for instance in a busy kitchen where a mother is also giving lunch to her older children—and if they receive a great deal of handling and holding at other times and are talked to and played with by a number of brothers and sisters as well as by their parents. It is only when the accompanying experiences and sensations are not provided at all that a baby is being neglected—starved, as it were, even while being fed.

Some parents are afraid they'll "spoil" their baby if they follow his cues in deciding when to feed him and how much. This fear is without any foundation. Perhaps it's time to reexamine the concept of "spoiling." The idea behind it seems to be that parents should accustom a baby to being given what *they* want rather than what he wants. Perhaps they fear losing control in a new and unknown and therefore unpredictable situation. But such a fear is not supported by the evidence we have of what babies are like.

You can't "spoil" a baby by giving him what he wants

at this age, because he's not really capable of wanting anything except what he needs—the comforts that reduce his tensions and restore his state of equilibrium. Later, when a baby begins to move around in his environment, the options open to him in the way of behavior increase with the growth of his intellectual capacities and his motor abilities. At that time it will become necessary to set limits and distinguish for him between what he may want to do and what he can actually be allowed to do. But it should simplify things for parents to realize that want and need are inseparable at the earliest stage of development.

Self-demand feeding does eventually become self-scheduling. Mothers needn't be afraid that self-demand feeding means they'll have to be ready, like short-order cooks, to serve up snacks at every hour of the day and night. Babies have a built-in physiological tendency to stabilize both their eating and their sleeping patterns, and as they get older they will eat larger amounts at less frequent intervals until, by the middle of their first year, they usually adapt quite naturally to a three-meal-a-day routine just as they do to sleeping through the night and taking a couple of naps during the day.

A rigid schedule of feeding by the clock may mean the baby sometimes is fed before he feels the desire for food, and sometimes eats only after his hunger pains have become intense and his tension has reached the level of violent crying and wild bodily activity. A meal under either of these conditions, as you know if you have ever tried to eat when you were not hungry or were feeling upset, is not likely to be a pleasant experience. On the other hand, mothers have many responsibilities, including the needs of their husbands and other children, as well as household tasks or outside work duties; this means they can't always feed a baby on a strictly demand basis. It's pointless for a mother to become so tense over a feeding situation, out of conviction that breast feeding or demand-schedule feeding will in itself be good for the baby, that she becomes resentful and irritable and inadvertently handles the baby in such a way that the mealtime becomes unpleasant.

The best solution is probably a compromise, a modified demand-feeding schedule, where a mother keeps track of the intervals at which her baby seems to get hungry and plans to feed him at around those times. Babies usually develop fairly regular hunger patterns of their own.

If an infant's tensions are relieved as they arise—if his needs for food, warmth, body contact and stimulation of his senses are met and he doesn't have to cry too long— he's getting the idea that the world is a good place to be and the people in it are worth getting to know. That's the most important goal of this stage of his development.

Some babies seem to linger over a feeding; others drain their bottles right down. It's important for parents to keep in mind how much each baby differs at birth in the rate and vigor of his sucking, and in the amount of food he requires, so they don't become anxious or impatient with a baby who is a slow eater, or upset if he eats less than they think he should.

While parents who feed bottled formula should try to see that their babies don't miss out on the pleasures of being held and touched and rocked and talked to, they needn't worry too much about the temperature of the bottle or of its contents. Studies have presented convincing evidence that a baby's physical and psychological well-being is in no way affected by being fed cold formula right from a refrigerator. It's possible that a mother's feeling that she should test for the "correct" temperature of the formula by seeing how a drop of it feels on her wrist may be an unconscious attempt to make the formula as much as possible like breast milk—which of course comes to the baby at the mother's body temperature.

All in all, it's not the specific feeding practice—breast or bottle, schedule or demand—that matters, but the context of the mother-child relationship in which the feeding takes place. The most thorough scientific attempts to date to compare the effects of breast feeding with those of bottle feeding suggest that it is impossible to reach any meaningful conclusion without reference to such factors as whether the babies were boys or girls, whether the mothers were warm or rejecting—in short, how the mothers felt about feeding their babies and how they handled them while doing so. What seems important is "the kind and amount of sensory and social stimulation a mother gives her baby, and her gratification of his needs."

Thus it would seem that a mother ought to choose to feed her baby in the way that makes for a pleasant situation for her and her baby—one in which they'll enjoy each other's company.

A mother who enjoys breast feeding probably feels more like a mother nursing her child. It reinforces her maternal feelings. In addition to benefiting nutritionally from human breast milk, the baby who is breast fed by a mother who enjoys doing so benefits from the cumulative effects of the pleasure their contact gives each of them during the feeding-time interaction between mother and child. But a mother who finds breast feeding unpleasant—whether because of her own upbringing, her husband's attitude, or the harassment of other children or other duties—probably does more harm than good by forcing herself to nurse her baby when she would find bottle feeding pleasanter or more convenient. The total experience of feeding, the amount of pleasure the baby gets from and gives to his mother, is what really counts.

If he's not hungry, a mother should feel free to put the

bottle aside and play with the baby and talk to him. Whether or not he has that last ounce won't matter as much as what kind of a feeling he has about the experiences the world offers and about those who offer them.

6

On Being a Parent

WHAT IS IT LIKE to be a parent? One thing we can say for sure is that it isn't always what one thought it would be like. Parents often feel differently about their children once they are actually on the scene than they thought they would in their plans and daydreams beforehand.

You may have carried around with you for half of your life the image of a plump smiling baby peacefully sleeping in your arms, only to find your newborn a wiry, tense little creature who seems to be howling most of the time. And you may never have pictured a beribboned and pina-fored two-year-old girl as a creature of grim defiance, shouting "No!" like a drill sergeant.

It will probably make you a better parent, not a worse one, if you're honest with yourself and accept your own feelings. All of them. You're bound to have some negative feelings toward your child once in a while. There *are* days when you wonder why you ever wanted to have children in the first place, and how are you going to get over the feeling if you don't start by acknowledging its existence? There's nothing wrong with facing up to the fact that once in a while your baby looks more like a member of another species than the child of your dreams, or that you have days when you'd rather be on a tropical island than changing diapers. This doesn't mean you're a monster; it only means you're a human being.

A baby's characteristics can effect a mother's feelings toward him—for example, whether he is cuddly or not, whether he seems to resemble her husband's nasty old uncle more than her own charming relatives, whether in general he fits in with her ideas of what a baby should be like, thus confirming that she is a good mother.

This is important to realize because how a mother feels about her child determines in great measure how she relates to him—how she handles him when he is very young and how she treats him when he is older. In fact, feelings often play a greater role than conscious beliefs or principles of child-raising. Thinking that parents should be "permissive," for instance, won't help you very much to decide how to respond in many particular situations. Should you try to protect a toddler from falls lest they discourage further attempts to move around on his own—or should you give him free rein to encourage his sense of mastery of his own movements? Two things have to be considered in any particular situation. One is the developmental processes which are taking place at this period of life. The other is the nature and needs of the particular child.

What we are saying is that you have to develop a rapport with your own child. This does not mean identifying yourself with him so that you feel what he feels, but retaining your parental role, which is to understand what he feels and give him what you think he needs. As he gets older, what he needs may not always be what he says he wants.

In effect, you have to be a parent for all seasons. In the

sense that it means providing what is best for the child in the long run, the parent's role remains constant for as long as the child needs parenting—that is, until he is grown up. In another sense, you have to keep changing constantly as a parent, depending on the child's changing developmental needs.

Many people find it much easier to be "baby" parents than to cope with school-age children. They are comfortable in the indulging role of the parents of young infants, but unable to bring themselves to set limits on these same children as they grow older. Others, whose natural bent for rules and order helps them to take a firm hand with older children, may be too rigid with young infants. We all know parents who seem to have done all the "right" things for their young infants—but never stopped doing these things, even when they were no longer the "right" responses for the child's age and he had begun to need to learn self-control and to handle a certain amount of frustration. Usually, the children of such parents are children one doesn't particularly like to have around—inconsiderate and destructive.

How you behave as a parent is a function of your own psychological style—your general approach to life and to other people. Your behavior as a parent is consistent with your behavior in other areas of life because it has its roots in the same soil of your own early experiences and responses to these experiences. The challenge of parenthood is to be able to shift from one kind of behavior to another as the child's needs change in the course of his development.

Only an understanding of the processes involved in the child's growth can guide you, along with your intuitive feelings, in deciding how to handle specific situations. Rules made according to other considerations may turn out to have quite different effects than you intended. This is what we might call the "squirrel effect" in child rearing. It's something like a man in the park throwing crumbs on the grass near a sign reading "Don't Feed the Pigeons" and protesting to a policeman, "But officer, I'm not feeding the pigeons. I'm feeding the squirrels."

As parents, we are sometimes feeding the pigeons when we think we are just feeding the squirrels. Thinking we are teaching a baby to be independent, we may in fact be teaching him to cling to infantile means of dealing with his discomforts that will only make him more dependent.

The good parent tries to do what will develop the child's ability to cope with circumstances for himself. The goal of doing things for a child should never be forgotten —it is not primarily for the pleasure you get out of doing things for him, or for the pleasure it gives him to have you do things for him, although both these things exist and play an important part. The goal is to enable him ultimately to do things for himself. In the end, it can be thought of as helping him to develop the capacity to plan ahead—to put off immediate gratification of his impulses and wishes for greater gratifications later on. All later ability to learn and to form meaningful relationships depends on this capacity.

Sometimes parents continue to gratify a child's early needs in a way that is no longer appropriate to his stage of development. They often prolong the use of a certain kind of comforting technique, instead of helping him learn to give it up when he is psychologically ready, because it is more convenient for them. They know he'll quiet down when he gets his pacifier and go off to sleep with no trouble for them.

Pacifiers, blankets and favorite soft toys often become objects of great importance to a child. These are the "transitional objects" that help him to shift from one type of activity, one situation or person, to another.

Change is hard for all of us. It requires a certain effort to adjust to any new situation, and it seems to be made easier if we can take with us something familiar from our previous life, just as immigrants moving to a new country bring with them objects from the "old country." A spoon, a picture, a piece of cloth, may have little intrinsic value and yet be priceless to the person who feels that in it he carries a little piece of home.

So the child who moves from waking to sleep, from one house to another, even from home to Grandma's or from being taken care of by mother to being looked after by a sitter for a few hours, has a desire to keep with him something that has come to be associated in his mind with comforting.

If a child has become dependent on a transitional object, whether it's his night bottle, what looks to you like a scrap of dirty old cloth, a rubber nipple or a stuffed rabbit that has seen better days, don't ask him to give it up unless he has something to take its place.

The something need not be a material object. The thing, after all, was originally a substitute for something else—mothering. In place of what you want him to relinquish, try offering him human contact—more time with you—or praise, through recognition that what he is doing is hard, confidence that he can manage it though, and admiration when he does. You can't expect to be able to take away something that has special meaning for him unless you substitute something else to meet the need he has.

The idea is to substitute something more appropriate, not something else that is equally inappropriate. For instance, buying something else for a child in place of an object like a pacifier or bottle—or even his own thumb—is not really replacing it at all. You may have exchanged one kind of material thing for another, but you are still encouraging him to be dependent on *things* to fulfill his emotional needs.

A better kind of solution might be to sit by his bed and tell him a story or read to him for a few minutes before he goes to sleep. That is substituting a relationship with a human being for emotional gratification through material things. We are not against things when they are used appropriately. Toys and books, records and objects of a million kinds, are invaluable materials for a child's perceptual, motor and intellectual development; but they shouldn't be relied on to meet his emotional needs. His need for something interesting to do should be met with various kinds of objects. His need for comfort should be met in the context of give and take with other people.

A young baby will accept a pacifier to suck on, but it may be more adaptive—more encouraging of growth and development—to satisfy his natural oral needs while feeding him, giving him the opportunity for eye-to-eye contact with his mother, holding him, letting him learn that pleasure comes from other people. But this is not to say it's "wrong" to use a pacifier or that you should never do so. As we have seen, babies differ greatly in physical characteristics of all kinds, and some seem to need much more sucking than others. No one would advise a mother to overfeed a baby who seems to need more sucking than he does food, or to stay at an infant's side to the exclusion of all other pleasures and responsibilities in her life.

But one general principle for these early months of a child's life might be to try not to give the child an object in place of yourself. The child needs you.

In the natural course of things, sucking becames a means of gratifying the child not only with food but also with closeness between him and his mother. The thing to watch out for, with bottles and with pacifiers, is encouraging the child to develop an attachment to an object he sucks on instead of to a person, as when he is breast fed. Then too, it is harder to wean a baby from these comforts than from the breast, perhaps because some natural process at work in mother and baby seems to taper off the mutual gratification of nursing at around the age a baby is usually able to learn to drink from a cup, some time in the last quarter of his first year. Some pediatricians think that it may be easier to begin weaning breast-fed babies directly to the cup at around eight or nine months than to take a bottle away from a baby the same age because the baby around this time develops a natural desire to be independent, to free himself from his mother physically and try to begin doing some things for himself. He may feel uncomfortable while being held at his mother's breast and be willing to learn to drink from the cup instead, whereas a bottle-fed baby at this age can just begin holding his own bottle and go right on drinking in the same old way without having to be encumbered by another person and by other arms in order to do so. He may thus have less motivation for learning to drink from a cup than the breast-fed baby.

7

Early Experience: The Key to Development

BEFORE WE MOVE on from thinking primarily about the needs of the very young infant to focusing on the next stage of life, let's sum up part of what we know about the behavior of human beings. All the recent scientific studies we have referred to have shown that in one way or another what happens very early in a child's life shapes his personality and contributes to the values, attitudes and behavior you will see in him later on. Research has taught us not only how vulnerable children are to early experience, but at what a very early age they begin to learn—in the first days of life, in some ways even before birth.

At first, most of an infant's movements are involuntary, inborn responses. If you place a finger or a rattle in a newborn's palm he will grasp it. If he is jarred suddenly he startles with his whole body, arching his back, throwing back his head and arms and clutching at the air. When placed in water he makes swimming movements with his arms and legs. At a touch near his mouth or on his cheek he purses his lips, moves his tongue and turns his head toward the side he was touched on, ready to find the nipple and suck. With the maturing of his brain and countless nerve pathways and with accumulated experience, the child gradually comes to control his own behavior. But in addition to the exercise of his sensory-motor apparatus, a very important kind of learning is taking place long before a baby can walk or talk or even do much more than cry and kick. What he is learning in these important early weeks and months is whether or not the world is a good place, whether the people taking care of him are worth loving and pleasing—whether to trust them.

During this early period some children will learn to withdraw from the world and the people in it. Some will fail to learn to cope with stress and be left with a tendency to be upset very easily by increased sensory stimulation. It appears that for such children, the predisposing factors of mental illness have been set down early in life. The other side of the coin is that what you do very early in a child's life can contribute positively to his emotional health and well-being.

Observations of other species of animals dramatically illustrate how its earliest experience can determine the direction an individual's development will take. Ducks and geese, for example, develop attachments to certain things in their environment within a short time after hatching. The first large moving object in a gosling's visual field within the early hours after it is hatched from its egg is the object it will attach itself to and follow around. Once that pattern has been established, it is impossible to reverse it. This is how the goose adjusts itself to its natural environment. Nature seems to have provided the living organism with a tendency to adapt itself to the environment into which it is born and it usually adjusts itself very quickly. Otherwise, it would not have the capacity to survive.

There seem to be genetic tendencies that the goose or

any living organism has to behave in a given way, but the immediate environment must stimulate or release these tendencies. The first environmental conditions it meets and must respond to determine the details of how the organism actually behaves. An example of how this works is the extent to which animals adapt to the food supply that is at hand. The first diet a rat is given—whether it is nutritionally adequate or not—is the diet it will select if given a choice later on in life. The animal tends to imprint itself to the conditions of its early environment and in a sense tries to remain in proximity with those conditions throughout its life.

This kind of learning probably exists to some degree at the human level too, although perhaps not as profoundly as in animals. We know there are periods of life in which a child is susceptible to the impact of certain experiences and not susceptible to others, and that you can establish certain response patterns, certain behavioral tendencies, during these critical early periods.

There are times in life when certain stimuli are necessary for the development of a pattern of behavior. If those stimuli are not present, the behavior will not develop. At the same time there are certain needs which, if they are frustrated, will persist and can never seem to be satisfied. The child will continue to have an insatiable desire, whether for sucking or cuddling or whatever meets that particular unsatisfied need. However, if you gratify these needs in early infancy while the baby is helpless and dependent on you—if you pick him up and hold him, carry him around and cuddle him, in addition to feeding him and keeping him warm and providing a variety of sights and sounds for him to respond to—then when his own feet begin to work, he'll be eager to go off on them. He'll want to be on his own, to be active and independent. Trying to force this independence too soon, in the first years of life, only encourages a child to cling to you even more.

The important thing is to provide the right experience at the right time. In the natural course of things, a newly hatched goose—through the instant learning process of imprinting—will fix on and follow its mother. Sometimes, though, if another moving object takes the mother's place, the young bird may become imprinted to it instead. This was the case with famed ethologist Konrad Lorenz, who described how newborn greylag geese accepted him as a mother substitute when he waddled around in front of them in place of their mother. It was a responsibility he could not shake off, since once the geese were imprinted —even to a distinguished scientist in place of a member of their own species—the attachment could never be broken or the process reversed Attachments thus formed by imprinting during the critical period following birth prove far more tenacious than responses learned by association to rewards or punishments. The greylag geese imprinted to Dr. Lorenz presumably went to their death still preferring him to any other living creature, even of their own kind. It is easy to see how such an attachment could make for a very maladaptive existence for a goose, who would fail to learn the things a goose has to know in order to survive and be quite unsuited for a relationship with any gander. It is also easy to see the value of this kind of learning—if the right stimulus is present at the right time.

If the stimulus is not present, and no imprinting takes place during the specific interval of the young animal's receptivity, imprinting can never take place at all. The animal avoids contact with others and cannot relate to them. The picture is strikingly similar to that of the infants raised in orphanages without sufficient handling or stimulation, who suffer from what has been described as "hospitalism," a condition of being withdrawn and unresponsive to other human beings.

It seems that maternal deprivation—the lack of sensory stimulation during the early weeks and months—can have a critical effect on the ability to form emotional attachments to other people later in life. We know that a duckling who is "negatively imprinted"—who isn't given the opportunity to form an attachment to its mother during the critical interval following birth—loses the capacity to form an attachment to her or to any other animal. It seems likely that in some way it may also be harmful to separate the human infant from his mother in the days just following birth when close physical proximity may be most essential to the development of a secure bond between them. It is at least worth considering the possibility that, failing to receive the needed stimulation at the critical time, an infant may suffer a major alteration in his responses—in extreme cases a permanent shutdown of his response mechanism whereby, like the duckling, he loses the ability to develop strong attachments.

Living things have two means of "knowing" how to behave.

Instinctive knowledge is information encoded in the genes of a species and passed down from one generation to another through the evolutionary process. Those chance mutations that work best—which enable an organism to survive and reproduce—tend to persist and to be transmitted to its offspring.

As distinct from these innate patterns of response to certain stimuli is the behavior which we learn through interaction with the environment, usually motivated by some system of rewards and punishments. We learn to do what makes us feel good—because we get fed, or earn praise, or avoid being hurt.

We don't know for sure how much of an infant's tendency to smile at a human face is innate and how much is learned by experience. But we can observe that there are certain stimuli which tend to strengthen the bond between the newborn infant and his mother. One of these seems to be the sound of the mother's heartbeat, a sound to which the infant has been exposed in the mother's body before birth, and which it must be soothing, comforting, somehow anxiety-reducing for him to continue to hear in the strange new surrounding in which he finds himself following birth. Try to imagine yourself having landed on a new planet after an immensely difficult voyage and you may get some idea of the reassurance that a familiar sound can give. It's as though you were able to take with you to Mars a portable radio, still broadcasting the sounds of home.

We can only surmise that the newborn baby misses the accustomed sound that was transmitted by the mother's aorta as it passed through the womb, and that he derives security from being held close to his mother's body, where he may hear—or feel—it again. But experimental evidence does show that this sound has a remarkably soothing effect on newborns. When amplified heartbeat sounds were played in a hospital nursery for newborns for the first four days of their lives, they cried less and gained more weight (probably because they used up less of their energy crying) than control babies who did not hear the heartbeat sound.

This certainly suggests that the sound of the maternal heartbeat reduces the anxiety or tension felt by the infant. Like the call of the mother duck, the sound of the mother's heartbeat signals her closeness. The maternal heartbeat may well operate as a kind of imprinting stimulus on the newborn baby He responds to it not by following her around, as the baby duck follows his mother, since the human newborn is relatively helpless and unable to move around by himself, but emotionally, by the relaxation of his tensions as he experiences comfort and security.

There is even some evidence to suggest that mothers have an unconscious, perhaps instinctive, tendency to hold their babies on the left side. Observations of human mothers as well as of rhesus monkeys have revealed a definite preference for the left side, regardless, in the case of the human mothers, of whether they were right-or left-handed. Without consciously thinking about it, a mother may intuitively feel that her baby is more comfortable held on her left side. And it gives her satisfaction too. A sensitive mother is pleased by the sensation of giving pleasure to her baby.

Interestingly enough, a survey of another field of human experience—works of art—reveals the same preference. In paintings and sculptures of mother and child from Italian Renaissance Madonnas to works by Henry Moore and Picasso, most of the mother figures are holding their infants on the left.

In literature too, as well as in our common speech, men use the word "heart" in expressing the feeling of love or closeness between people. Anatomically we know the emotions are controlled by a part of the brain called the hypothalamus, and not by the heart. Yet you never hear anybody say, "I love you from the bottom of my hypothalamus." In all forms of poetry in all languages and throughout the ages, men have used the word "heart" when speaking of feelings of attachment to other human beings. Perhaps this way of expressing pleasure in closeness to others has its origins in the universal prenatal experience of the mother's heartbeat sound and the pleasure it gives the newborn baby to hear it continuing.

It is even possible that the universal appeal of music is based on the early association of the rhythm of the human heartbeat with feelings of pleasure, imprinted during prenatal life. Music and dance may represent an attempt to remain in proximity with imprinted stimuli, with the constant repetitive sensation which stops when the baby is born. In most music, from the primitive beating of drums to Beethoven's late string quartets, the tempo ranges between 50 and 150 beats per minute—essentially the range of the human heartbeat.

Because of the persistence of certain basic response patterns established very early in life, when we talk about infancy we are also talking about the problems of later childhood, adolescence, the young adult and the aging person. All of them are foreshadowed in infancy. It has become clear in the experience of countless psychiatrists, psychologists, psychoanalysts, social workers and scientists in every field of human behavior in our century that how the child loves determines how he will love as an adult.

Clinical experience also shows how difficult it is to change early behavior patterns once established. It would seem that our best hope for a better world—one in which more people love than hate—lies in doing what we can to prevent emotional illness from the very beginning of life. Having done so, having made a helpless infant happy and secure by responding to his needs, brings one a step closer to the parent's ultimate gratification: a happy and self-sufficient person—one who is able to love and to work. If your baby's earliest needs are gratified, chances are that he will face the world at a year with the spirit of an enthusiastic explorer—with curiosity about what it's all like out there, and confidence that it's worth trying to find out.

As he moves into the second years of life, a child takes two giant strides forward into individuality. One is being able to move around on his own. The other involves the acquisition of language, the ability to use symbols to deal with abstract thought that makes us such unique animals.

Civilization now enters the picture. In a way, the mother's role now shifts subtly from an extension of natural evolution to a cultural force. Her job now is to encourage those behavior patterns which make it possible for the child to take his place in human society. In the next section we will see how this process takes place.

PART 2

After Infancy:
The Baby Becomes
a Child

8

Learning to Be a Person: The First Steps

WE HAVE SEEN how the helpless infant of the early months of life gradually learns to be responsive to the world of other people. Learning more about that world and how to function in it becomes his next task as he moves toward the end of his first year.

In this chapter we'll describe some of the child's behavior patterns at this stage and their relation to the growth process. Then, in the remaining chapters of this section, we'll discuss in greater detail the interrelated processes of language development, play, discipline, feeding and toilet training, and relationships with others, describing the kinds of problems that often occur and suggesting what kinds of solutions are most useful in encouraging growth and preventing serious emotional disorders.

What is the baby like as he approaches the end of his first year and moves toward toddlerhood?

As he becomes able to move around and do more things, he becomes more capable of aggressive behavior. If no one stops him, he will bite, break, spill and tear, attacking playmates, toys, and even himself with equal gusto. He can be quite destructive, even self-destructive, unless he is helped to cope with his aggression by parents who help him, as he explores his environment, to see what's there and learn how to deal with it in a constructive way.

This is the foundation of the individual's personality and value system. If this learning is bypassed now, it can never really be made up. No psychiatrist can put back what is missing from early development. This is not to minimize the help that psychiatry can offer troubled people, but only to emphasize the crucial importance of trying to prevent emotional disturbance from the beginning of life instead of having to deal with it later.

When a school child cannot concentrate, a young adult cannot keep a job or has difficulty expressing love or tenderness, or an old person cannot get along with others, we can usually see how these difficulties relate to early life experiences, such as how they were stimulated, or fed, or disciplined, perhaps as newborns, as babies, as two-year-olds. It is far easier to influence the outcome of personality by the way one handles children early in life than to change behavior patterns once they already exist in a teenager, a young adult or a parent.

The young child is involved in the processes of learning to cope and learning to love, and they are intertwined. A sense of being able to do things contributes, along with the sense that he is valued by others who seem important, to his self-esteem. If he does not have a good relationship with others whom he wants to please, he'll have no motive for learning what they are prepared to teach him. And if he can't handle his aggressive and destructive impulses, he will be rejected by others and have a much harder time forming satisfying relationships.

If he has learned to respond to people, the child has begun by now to select the people he will respond to. He smiles at familiar faces and cries when strangers approach him. He has learned to differentiate people.

He has already learned to associate smiling with pleasure. He still takes almost everything into his mouth as one way of exploring it. Now he has teeth and he often has a tendency to bite with them. He begins to learn that biting hurts, that other people have feelings like his. A mother who lets her baby bite her or hit her without saying "ouch" and indicating her displeasure in her face and voice is failing to teach her baby something he ought to learn. (And the person who finally teaches him this particular lesson may be a far less gentle teacher than she is!)

The child also has a tendency to want to continue any activity he's engaged in, to follow it through uninterruptedly. The satisfaction gained in following through on a sustained interest is self-rewarding. It is unpleasant to be interrupted and can lead the child to a pattern of behavior that involves avoidance of anything that may take a long time to complete because he doesn't want to have to face the prospect of being taken away from doing something he likes. This feeling that it's just not worth getting started on something he won't be allowed to finish can be a factor in his later lack of ability to initiate tasks or to concentrate on them.

At first the baby used his whole body in play. He seems to act just for the sake of the activity itself, doing just to be doing, moving just to feel himself move. Only gradually does he come to observe the effects of his actions on the world around him and begin to perform these actions with some definite goal in mind. After his aimless swipes of the arm have knocked over a pillow a few times, he begins to take an interest in the pillow's fall and to move his arm *in order* to see the pillow fall.

He is learning to do things to the environment that

causes the environment to do things back. He will often become irritable in the face of the inevitable frustrations he meets as he tries to get around on wobbly legs or get ahold of some tantalizing object just out of reach. He is testing all his abilities, and he can't distinguish aggressive and destructive actions from other behavior without some guidance. He has to be taught that it might be all right to touch, but not to throw. A parent's job is to help him find for himself constructive ways of relating to and operating in the world of people and things.

A boundless curiosity accompanies the child's increased capacity to learn; the trick is not to interfere with it but to channel it. Providing him with many different kinds of things to feel, to move, to push and pull, open and close, listen to and look at, gives him opportunities to explore the world of things around him and find out what effects he can produce on it. "No" will be easier for him to learn if you save it for the important things where it really counts and where you really mean it—things that burn or cut or are in some other way dangerous. In other situations it is often a good idea to distract him with something else that's more acceptable. The point is to avoid restricting him unnecessarily, but not to avoid restricting him at all. When you do say "no," you should mean it, and he should know that you do.

He will try to do many things you don't want him to do—pull the cat's tail, smear his food in his hair, turn his glass of milk upside down, knock the receiver off the telephone—and one way for him to learn what he can't do is by trying it. *Then* you can teach him not to. Having the experience, and then being corrected, he learns what he can and can't do. And he learns partly because he wants to be like you and to please you. This is the basis for his eventually developing a conscience of his own—an internal set of rules for what should and should not be done.

Unless this process of internalization takes place he'll be like a dog who lies on the sofa all day while you're away but jumps off the minute you come home. He hasn't learned not to sit on the sofa; he's learned not to sit on the sofa when you're around. In other words, he's learned not to get caught. The lesson learned was not about the substance of the rules but about the punishment for getting caught breaking them.

What's missing in this state of things—whether it's the baby lunging for the cat when your back is turned or the delinquent who steals cars—is a strong identification with those who make the rules—the feeling that it's *his* rule, a feeling which has as its original basis the desire to be like you who made it. Even as babies, what we feel is a good thing is what we want to have for ourselves, and even as very young children we pattern ourselves on those we love, those who gratify us, meet our needs and help us—those we trust. We try to take on their characteristics and imitate their behavior. A parent who has pretty consistently helped his child to cope with his environment is a parent the child will feel protected by and will want to be with. And one way of being with someone even when he is not present is to try to be like him one's self. This process of identification with a parent he has learned to trust in the early months of life is the basis for the child's socialization now.

Two things are essential for this process to take place. The child has to have experience to learn from, and a certain amount of frustration—not enough to overwhelm him and repress his curiosity, but enough to mobilize him to try to do something about the frustration. Children whose parents always try to keep them away from experiences in which they might do any damage have little opportunity to learn the results that doing damage can have. These are the "good" model children who are inflexible because they haven't learned to adapt by coping with real situations and who may have difficulty generalizing from one experience to another. They seem brittle—tightly held in check—and easily explode. They don't think for themselves or follow their own set of rules but follow a leader blindly. This is the authoritarian personality, which seems to flourish in cultures where young children are kept immaculately clean and tidy, are prevented from experiencing very much through their own manipulation of their environment, and are overwhelmed by strict, punitive authority figures. The trick—and all good educators know this, whether they educate as parents or as teachers—is not to punish but to discipline.

Some parents don't know when to stop gratifying their children. There are two extremes—all love and all punishment, the all-giving and the punitive parent figure—and both can contribute to the formation of a disturbed child.

While you don't want to overpower the child in enforcing your will, you do have to let him know what your will is. Much of the time he is testing you, doing things and looking to see what your reaction will be. Your tone of voice and facial expression have communicated your feelings to him up to now; now they begin to be associated with certain words as well: "No!" for one. This is the forerunner of learning the meaning of various words.

In the second year of life the baby is not only growing physically, he is moving from infancy toward childhood. The formerly almost totally dependent infant is developing an increasing drive toward independence and autonomy. He is becoming aware of himself as a separate person and he wants to do things by and for himself. He is beginning to learn what he can do with his own body, as well as a little about the other people and things in his environment.

The crucial process of the early months of life was for

the baby to learn that he could depend on his environment to help him. Now, in the next phase of his development, he has to learn that he can help himself.

It's a vitally important thing for parents to keep in mind at this stage of a child's development that he has to learn to do things for himself, even though it may mean more trouble for you at the moment. In the long run, it's worth the extra time and trouble now waiting for him to struggle into his own galoshes rather than giving in to the temptation to grab them yourself so you can get it over with and get on to the store. The clinical evidence suggests that many children who later show great dependency and an unwillingness to do things for themselves have been conditioned by a parent's constant tendency to do things for them.

The adolescent who never seems to be able to assume any household or family responsibilities is often the one who at an early age was not encouraged to help out with some jobs and then rewarded for it. Even having a two-year-old go to the door for the morning newspaper and be rewarded with a smile and "I'm proud of you" can create an indelible impression. That two-year-old may even resent someone else doing "his job," an indication that he's not only taken on responsibility but has a sense of self-esteem. The parent who ignores this may be giving up a valuable opportunity to prevent the kinds of problems that sometimes arise in adolescents and young adults with regard to family and social responsibilities.

Your praise needn't be overwhelming. A word of quiet approval can do a child more good than grossly exaggerated reactions to his every accomplishment. If you do handsprings every time a child picks up a crayon and makes a line, he may become accustomed to, and need, a degree of praise for everything he does which you'll probably find hard to maintain and which the rest of the world is hardly likely to bestow on him. He'll be doing things more for the praise he gets than for any intrinsic pleasure in the task itself.

The child's new drive for independence leads to a number of practical problems. It will help you solve them if you keep in mind the main developmental goal of this period of his growth and then find the solution that works best in your home or on your schedule or with your family and that is also consistent with his need to learn to act for himself and to do so within the general limits approved by society.

Over the months, the baby will go from creeping and crawling to walking unsteadily and then to investigating things as he moves around. He's like an explorer in a new country, understanding little of the natives, not speaking the language, not knowing what the local dangers are. You have to help him sort them out, and also to learn how to do the sorting for himself. In a sense, you have to equip him for later voyages of discovery he'll make alone, without your help.

Rather than forbidding him too many things or caging him in a playpen, it is a good idea to try to channel his new abilities to move and act in ways that permit him to experience a sense of mastery and learn certain limits at the same time. Instead of "No, no, don't get dirty, don't make a mess," it might be "You can't make the living room dirty but you can mess with this finger paint all you want, try all the things you can think of, as long as you stay on the paper here in the kitchen."

In the course of learning to do so many new things and accept inevitable limitations, the toddler is bound to feel frustrated sometimes. It's probably a good idea to let him feel angry as long as he does what's asked. You can expect a child to do what you say—that's your right as a parent. But you can't always expect him to be happy about it—that's his right as an individual with feelings of his own. You can require him to limit his expressions of anger to words or facial expressions, but not to suppress them altogether. The baby can't kick you or hit you because you won't let him pour the sugar on the floor but he *can* cry or say "Bad Mommy," just as when he's eight he can't take away his sister's piece of cake because he thinks it's larger than his but he *can* grumble and insist "That's not fair!" and just as when he's fifteen and has to clean up the yard he's entitled to sulk about it—as long as he does it.

Sometimes we parents are so concerned about our children's love—about the gratification we get from their expressions of affection to us—that we let that need of ours determine our behavior toward them instead of being guided by what their long-range needs are. In the end, though, our children will appreciate us for how well we have equipped them for their life, not how many lollipops or toys we gave them at the moment they wanted them. And, like our children, we parents too have to be able occasionally to postpone the immediate gratification of a child's present approval of us for the greater gratification of his approval when he is older—and understands more.

Of course we're not suggesting you be mean to your child! We *are* suggesting that if you are sure that a certain course is good for him—that it's what he needs at this stage of his development—you needn't be afraid of losing his love. That fear should neither cause you to change your course nor to try to keep him from expressing and acknowledging his negative feelings about it—and even occasionally about you—as long as he does not act these feelings out destructively. In fact, you do him a useful service if you teach him to come to grips with aggressive feelings and destructive wishes and deal with them verbally or channel them in some other socially acceptable way. If you encourage him to deny their very existence, they'll only crowd him internally until they finally break out in some undesirable way. A useful principle to follow with children is "You have to do it—but you don't have to like it." Kids have an inalienable right to grumble.

9

Learning and Language

THE CHILD'S NEW THRUST toward independence is made possible by two important changes around the end of the first year of life, the ability to move around on his own, and the acquisition of speech. He is beginning to play with words as well as things.

At a certain stage all babies begin to babble and make various kinds of sounds. If no response is forthcoming, they stop, just as they give up smiling if no one smiles back at them at the critical time. Parents stimulate language development by responding to a baby's babbling, just as earlier they responded to his cries when these were his only means of communication. Usually, they do so instinctively, for the pleasure it gives them. Again, as with smiling and crying, this seems to be a natural process of interaction by which the parent stimulates certain capacities in the child.

When babies begin to babble, mothers seem to have a natural tendency to encourage them to imitate speech sounds and, eventually, words. Mothers usually enjoy "talking" to their infants, and the baby's response, his effort to imitate the sounds she makes, delights a mother. Her love and approval lead him to repeat these efforts to make sounds like words, then to reproduce the rhythm and intonation of speech, eventually to say real words and, finally, to use words correctly. In this way a responsive mother, whose delight in her child's accomplishments means love and pleasure for him, stimulates his language development.

A problem in some families is a tendency to anticipate a child's wants instead of letting him communicate them. It's important to give children a chance to let you know what *they* want, and then respond to this. If you answer all their calls, and communicate with them without their having to use words, what's the point of learning to talk? This is why you find some normal children who are quite delayed in speech development—simply because there's no need for it.

By encouraging him to repeat the sounds he makes and to "speak" back to them, parents show him that others respond to his voice and that he can use it to communicate with, more and more precisely. He learns that while a cry will get him something to eat, the word "cookie" will get him the specific thing he wants.

Studies have shown that infants raised in orphanages vocalized less frequently and made fewer kinds of sounds than those raised in families at home, probably because their first efforts met with no response and there was no one they were attached to and wanted to imitate. The evidence clearly shows that language development depends to a great extent on environmental stimulation, not just maturation.

Language games have delighted mothers and babies ever since speech became a human characteristic. The tendency most mothers have to talk to their babies is an adaptive one—one that serves to stimulate the child's development. The pleasure children take in rhythm, in repetition and alliteration, in the sound—and sometimes it almost seems the *taste* of words—explains the universal appeal of all the old nursery rhymes, of "Hey diddle diddle" and "Hickory dickory dock."

A number of recent studies in which mothers in disadvantaged groups were given books and instructed in how to make use of them have shown how much increased stimulation can affect the level of speech development. Mothers of an experimental group of babies between one year and two and a half years old spent just fifteen minutes a day looking at picture books with them, pointing out objects in the pictures and naming them, reading stories aloud and talking about them. At two and a half these children were far more advanced in their speech than those in a control group without the extra stimulation.

A child who is learning to talk needs objects—a whole range and variety of materials and playthings—to name and talk *about*. He needs different colors, shapes, textures, sounds, to stimulate his interest and encourage his perception of differences. Toys don't "spoil" a child unless they are given to him for the wrong reasons.

The toddler is beginning to change from responding only to sensorimotor stimuli—sensations and movement —to behaving in response to verbal stimuli—words and phrases. He needs a chance to see and feel what is being named. Much of the interaction between parent and child in the second year of life consists of word play—labeling things and learning to identify them by name. A little later on, in the third year, he will begin to use some conceptual words, words like "heavy" that are not names of things but express abstract ideas or qualities. But he won't understand what they mean unless he has a chance to learn them in the context of experience, picking up a box and feeling the pull in his muscles as you say "heavy." This is one way he learns more about his environment. The ability to express his understanding of things through language enables him to be corrected and little by little to put together a reliable picture of the world around him. A little girl we know was about three when her father picked her up and said, "You're not as light as you used to be!" "I guess," she replied, "I must be getting darker."

The acquisition of language also helps to define the boundaries of self and make him aware of the individuality of other people. ("Me" and "You" come into use along with "Mommy" and "Johnny.") He names himself and other people as well as the things around him. Learning to differentiate the objects in his environment is easier when he can label them, and perceiving the distinctions between different things enables him to act on them more effectively, to plan, and to make better use of them. The labeling process is really enjoyable to children. They take great pleasure in learning how to use words. If it is interfered with, not encouraged at this stage, the child may have trouble in learning later on.

A preschool child gets a great kick out of telling you a story and having you write it down and read it back to him. He gets some sense of logical construction, of the sequence of ideas. He can make use of your skill in writing, which he's not yet able to do for himself, and this helps stimulate his desire to learn to write himself.

The two capacities of movement and language give the child more flexibility in the world. The development of speech helps facilitate the ability to control his impulses. He can substitute words for action. At one he can say "no" instead of kicking or biting, just as at five he can say "I hate you!" instead of hitting or hurling something.

In a sense, when the child learns to name things, this labeling ability gives him a new power over them. He can refer to things and he can "manage" them mentally even when they are not present before him. With the acquisition of language and the realization that things continue to exist even when he cannot see or hear or touch them, he begins to be capable of abstract thought. And the dawning knowledge of the continuing existence of things beyond his immediate sensing of them also helps him to cope increasingly well with short separations from his mother.

Babies learn, after many games of peekaboo and hide-and-seek, that things which go away come back, as well as that things may disappear from sight and still be somewhere.

Language opens the world beyond the child's physical perceptions. It also enables him to communicate with others, to relate to them. He can let them know how he feels and learn how they feel by means of language at the same time that he is trying out new kinds of behavior. He learns that certain things he does make others feel good —or bad—and this in turn influences how they treat him.

What about the "early learning" of elementary-school skills so many parents have come to think they should teach at home?

A child who's secure in a friendly world and exposed to a variety of objects and stimulations is learning all the time. The key word here is "exposed"—not forced. He learns in all his play. He's constantly observing, comparing, relating, trying, testing, concluding. The most useful thing parents can do to help him be ready for school is probably just to keep him in a frame of mind in which he is receptive to experience—interested in the world—and make experience available. He'll do the rest himself as a natural process at this age. He'll probably even begin asking about letters and numbers as he observes them everywhere around him—on houses, on packages, on the television screen. Answering his questions as he asks them, to the extent of his interest, keeps that interest going. Sitting down to give him a formal course in reading may not have that same effect.

Providing a young child with learning experiences doesn't necessarily mean structuring his time in "educational" activities recommended for instant I.Q.-boosting. Picture books and records, trips to the zoo or just to a friend's house, going to a museum or to the supermarket are all bound to be learning experiences as long as they're a pleasure for both of you and you are responsive to his interest in what he sees.

When he's an adolescent he may have temporary difficulty learning because of his inner turmoil, bombarded as he is bound to be some of the time by new and disturbing feelings. Teenagers can often benefit a good deal from structured situations that help them channel their energies. But the child of preschool age is eager to question the world. He greets every new face or place like a challenge to be gotten to the bottom of ("What's that?" "Where did it come from?" "Who's that man?" "What's he doing?") and he will go on asking "why" indefinitely. You don't have to shovel knowledge into him; he'll rush out to gather it up if given the opportunity.

Ask yourself who is doing the more important learning —the four-year-old squirming on the sofa while his father teaches him letters of the alphabet to impress the teacher at the nursery school he's applying to or the one who is out walking with his father, making a game out of identifying different makes of cars on the street, talking about what's in the store windows they pass.

In the end, attitude can be a more important ingredient of reading readiness than the alphabet.

Parents who set out to teach their young children to read or do arithmetic because they feel they want to give them an early start, often disrupt a sequence in development and interfere with the relationship between parent and child, which is not to be confused with the teacher-student relationship. It is not uncommon for children whose parents have persisted in efforts to teach them the alphabet or numbers to develop an aversion to learning because of this parental pressure. The parent's major role is loving and protecting, and a child in this situation may come to confuse this with learning and to feel that he may lose his parents' love unless he conforms to their academic expectations.

It's one thing to answer a child's question about the numbers he sees on the street signs or the letters printed on the sides of trucks and to offer him as much information as he really seems to want, and something else again to structure efforts at teaching reading or number skills into the day of a preschooler. The pressure may actually make him *less* ready for school. A better basis for doing well in the classroom is a combination of interest in the world, including its signs and symbols, that hasn't been squelched by pressure, together with a good feeling about his own capability, that hasn't been overtaxed to the point of self-doubt. That, and a security in the knowledge that you love him. The teacher doesn't have to love him in order to teach him, as long as he knows that you love him, and he will find it easier to learn from his teacher if he doesn't begin to confuse your loving with his learning.

10

Learning to Play

AS HE MOVES OUT into the world, the baby moves from playing with his own body to playing with other objects, his toys. Gradually, he will move from a child's play to a man's work, and much of how we are able to work is determined by how we once played.

At first, the baby's pleasures came from mouthing his fingers and touching his own skin and his mother's, which, in the beginning at least, he didn't distinguish from his own. His first plaything was probably some stuffed animal or other soft object which felt like his own and his mother's body and by its familiarity helped him feel secure as he made the transition from sleep to wakefulness, or from being with mother to being alone or with someone else. Then he began to like various other soft toys as well as other kinds of play materials, no longer so much for their emotional content but as the means of developing his own ego, his own sense of controlling his own body and mastering his environment. Now he begins to use toys primarily to learn ways of coping with things.

In the very beginning, toys were stimulators of his sensorimotor apparatus. Mobiles to look at, music boxes to listen to, rag dolls to touch and feel, rubber rings to gum on, taste and chew and smell. In a stimulus-rich environment, the more he perceived the more he was able to respond to and the more he craved in the way of stimulation. In addition, there was the emotional meaning of certain playthings.

As he begins to move around and develop better motor coordination, his play, which is really his work throughout childhood, enables him to exercise his muscles as well as his imagination, to find out how things work and how he can work them. In short, he learns what effects he can have on his environment. He does this by pushing and pulling, opening and shutting, taking out and putting in, building up and knocking down.

In the beginning of this phase he enjoys these activities purely for their own sake. Then he begins to engage in them purposely for the effect he has observed they produce—for a result. When he does something for the sake of an end product, he is on the way to being able to learn and to work. He is learning to be able to complete a task, to solve a problem. This, together with a desire to please the adults from whom he learns—first his parents and later his teachers—is the basis for doing well in school. We hesitate to say for "achievement," because of a suspicion that scholastic achievement, as measured by tests and grades, is not always a reliable indicator of what we are talking about, which is the ability to learn from experience and to apply that knowledge in new situations.

The child this age has a real need for play materials he can handle and manipulate, move around and change, just as when he was younger he had a need for things to look at and listen to, touch and feel. This does not mean they have to be expensive commercial toys, or prepackaged "programed play experiences." Often these cost as much as they do because of the advertising or packaging involved. (We know a few children who are discerning enough to prefer the handsome box in which a rather disappointing toy is misleadingly packaged, and to make out of it a tractor, pirate ship or doll bed. Sometimes in the course of a single afternoon, a really good cardboard box can be all three.)

Any toys will do, or any household implements. Babies and young children love to play with "real" things—bunches of keys and flashlights, pots and pans, eggbeaters and wooden cooking spoons from the kitchen, pocketbooks and hats from the closet. These things have the added attraction of belonging to Mommy and Daddy—or being just like the ones that do—and make it easier for the child's imagination to bridge the gap between the reality of his being small and the pretense of being big that is such an important part of learning what it's really like to be big.

Because play is such an important part of learning, and because the process of learning who he is depends so much on learning what he can do, parents should try to provide children with as much as they can in the way of toys and play materials. But objects should be provided as things he needs to grow on, like his meals, and not mixed up with unnecessary emotional meaning.

What this means is that toys shouldn't be used for disciplinary purposes, as rewards or as substitutes for your attention. They shouldn't be given to him because he's "good," or because you're going to go out and leave him with a sitter; they should be given to him because he has a developmental need which they satisfy.

The child benefits enormously from a stimulus-rich environment. At first that means things that move, things that he can see and hear. As he gets a little older it means a chance to be able to alter his environment—that is, to be able to affect his world, to change things in it at his own will. If the child is always at the mercy of his environment, if he never has a chance to influence it by his own manipulation, by moving things around, he develops a sense of passivity. Children who are beginning to explore the world around them feel a greater sense of security about their environment when they find they can change it. For instance, a two-year-old may want to move a chair for no particular purpose; it just gives him a great sense of accomplishment to be able to do so.

It's also important to let a child listen to music and look at pictures, to give him toys of different textures to play with, toys he can handle and move around and change.

But it defeats their purpose as stimuli once you begin to use toys as rewards, to say, "If you're good, you can have this or that." After all, toys and play materials for our children are what books and records are for us. We need them for our own mental stimulation. Wouldn't you be bored without them? Toys do more than keep children from being bored, though. Play is how they learn, how they develop spatial relations and a feel for color, for instance.

Toddlers have new physical abilities and aggressive tendencies, and parents have to help them curb their aggression and learn to channel it into socially acceptable behavior, such as running and throwing games, splashing and bouncing play.

There are some parents who labor under the misapprehension that if they interfere with anything their child wants to do they will somehow stunt his emotional or intellectual growth. The child has certain needs, including the need to feel an increasing mastery of his own body as well as of his environment, but another of his needs is to learn to control his own impulses and not to infringe on the rights of other people. Civilization depends on a certain degree of restraint on everyone's part, on no one's riding roughshod over the rights of others. One of the things we must begin to learn as children is that it's not a "free country" in the sense that you can do anything you feel like doing at any time. People who fail to learn this wind up with no regard for the integrity of others.

If a child walks into your house and writes on your walls and breaks your ashtrays, your first thought is bound to be, "I don't want this kid back in my house again," and chances are you won't readily invite his parents back either.

What these parents have done is create a situation in which their child is likely to be rejected. A child who is able to have fun spontaneously and at the same time control his destructive impulses and show a certain regard for manners is not only going to be more readily accepted but will in a sense have much more freedom of activity because more options will be open to him socially. He will have developed patterns of behavior that are worthwhile in terms of making adaptations in adulthood.

Many people seem to think that if you limit a child's freedom of action you are taking away his creative ability. They fail to distinguish between that which is creative and that which is destructive. There are even educators who don't make that distinction. They think that if a child throws something against a wall, it's a work of art, and if it hits three people on the way, that has nothing to do with it. But that's not art—it's an accident that occurred in the process of a destructive act. Anything we can really call art involves a certain degree of conscious selection as well as the patience to persist at an activity until a desired effect can be achieved. And anything we can really call play involves a certain awareness of the effects of one's actions on the materials or the other people involved, and a degree of restraint regarding those effects.

Very young children don't really play with each other at first. In fact, they hardly seem to realize the existence of other children as creatures like themselves. They seem to think of them as things, objects which are sometimes a convenience (you can grab for a ball they brought with them), sometimes a nuisance (they interfere with things by taking away Mother's attention). Repeated exposures —involving the experience of a certain resistance at the other end when the ball is grabbed—reveal the fact that those objects are creatures like themselves, who also hurt when they are hit (evidence: they howl) and even hit back (so perhaps one shouldn't?).

In these earliest contacts with others—those his own age as well as the grownups who take care of him—the child establishes certain patterns of social behavior that will persist through life. If he is going to be able to share with his brothers and sisters, then take turns with his schoolfellows, and eventually cooperate with his colleagues in whatever work he does, he has to begin getting some sense of the existence, needs and feelings of other people now.

By helping children develop controls over their own destructive urges to the person and property of others, parents help them to become the kind of people others want to be with. They increase the likelihood that their children will find other people rewarding and will grow up with the idea that life is for living with them.

Many of the destructive people, the killers, the assassins we've come to know in our society have been "loners"— people who have had no close relationships with others. It is on the basis of such attachments formed very early in life that character is developed, and the time to start is now, at the very beginning, not when they are adolescents. By then it is too late.

It's a real question whether it serves any purpose to do away with toy guns or whether we ought to concentrate instead on doing away with the tendency to have strong destructive feeelings toward others and to act on these impulses.

You needn't overpower a child just because you establish certain limits. It's possible to show him that you are pleased he can do some things by himself and can go off by himself sometimes, but that there are other times when you have to do things for him or with him. You'll tell him when they are but at those times you want him to listen to you and do things your way.

Children should have the opportunity to express themselves—with the limitation that they don't infringe upon the rights of others and limit *their* freedom in expressing themselves.

Whenever you can eliminate conflict between a parent and a young child, it's a worthwhile thing to do. There's always a certain loss of face in a confrontation, whether it's the child's pride or your pride that's involved.

You can teach children a great deal by demonstration. There is nothing sillier than a mother screaming at her child for not being well behaved. She is doing what she is telling him not to do. Think of it from the child's point of view; he can have his feelings hurt too. If you tell him, for instance, that you are annoyed with him for misbehaving earlier but you didn't want to say so in front of other people and so you waited until you were alone to tell him, he will learn a little about social sensitivities that he can incorporate into his own character.

It's a good idea to help the child think about his behavior in terms of the effects it has, rather than using expressions like "good" and "bad" which imply some absolute. In a sense you're taking away from the child his own right to make a decision when you say, "This is good and that's bad," or "You're a good boy or a bad boy." It's more useful to say to the child, "It makes me feel good— or unhappy—when you do things like that," or "It makes people uncomfortable when you act that way, and it bothers me when I see you do it." This doesn't make him feel guilty or worthless.

Most of the time a child's feelings of guilt are associated with something more deep-rooted than the overt behavior you see—with his fantasies of forbidden experiences or his secret desires. If you tell him he's bad because he won't share his toys, you may actually be confirming his own secret thought that he is bad because of some other, hidden, thoughts or wishes you're not aware of. It is quite common for a child to entertain thoughts that involve terrible things happening to a parent or getting rid of his sisters and brothers, so he can have all his mother's attention for himself.

If the child recognizes that he can elicit a reaction from you in positive as well as negative ways, he learns that he can influence the behavior of other people, that he can change his own social environment just as he can his physical surroundings. Part of the tragedy of our time seems to come from the fact that so many people feel they have relatively little capacity to change their own environment in positive ways. It's oppressive at any age to feel you're completely at the mercy of forces beyond your control.

Think of a little child who's in the hospital. He can't really do anything about his situation except cry. When the time comes for him to be given some nasty-tasting medicine or a painful injection or to undergo some frightening series of diagnostic procedures, he knows that no matter what he says, "they" are going to do it. Those people in the white coats are bigger and stronger than he is and they're in charge.

The child's feeling of helplessness must be overwhelming, and hospitalized children very often seem to experience something close to despair, especially when they are too young to really understand why their parents have left them there.

It's important for children in a hospital situation to feel that in some way they can affect their own situation, that someone responds to their cries or that they can control something—perhaps a toy or a mobile they can move—at their own will. This seems to give them a feeling that they are not totally the victim of outside forces and that they can alter their environment in some way in order to obtain some degree of pleasure.

In the same way, healthy children at home, when they feel that they can have some influence on your behavior, learn to interact with other people and acquire a greater sense of self-esteem—what is called "ego." What you're doing in this way is helping the child learn ways of coping with the world, ways of dealing with his own anxieties and the inevitable feelings of guilt related to fantasies everyone has at various developmental periods. He learns ways of behaving that effectively diminish his tensions and discomforts.

If you begin to establish this kind of interaction now, the child can use those patterns of behavior later. As a mature individual, he'll have a larger repertoire of resources for dealing with stress and tension. He'll be better able to adapt to the unexpected and less easily overwhelmed by pressures.

The principle to keep in mind in thinking about discipline is that you have to deal with a child in terms of his capacity to understand. Young children are confused by some of the things we say to them. For one thing, they have little understanding of time sequence. When you say to a very young child, "If you do that you can't watch television tomorrow," well, tomorrow doesn't even exist for him clearly yet. It's more useful to put it on the basis of your feelings about what the child is doing. If you say, "I'm very annoyed with you" and your face and voice show this, the child will be concerned. That's usually enough—just letting him know how you feel. By the same token, when he's doing something you like, if you're enthusiastic about it and show you're pleased with him, this is a far more constructive way of guiding his behavior than saying to a child, "If you're good you can have this," or "If you're bad I'm going to take that away." All you're teaching a child when you do that is how to negotiate with material objects, and when he's twenty years old and he's flunking out of college he'll come to you and say, "If you'll buy me a sportscar . . ."

If from the very beginning you communicate that you have feelings about what your child does, he learns rules and limits at the same time that he learns to relate to other people, not to things, for his emotional needs. At this stage, if he has learned to trust you, your child wants very much to be loved by you, to be accepted by you, and not to make you angry, because if you're in a bad mood you're not friendly to him, you don't play with him, and all the pleasures he associates with you are diminished.

This seems to be a much better method than using material objects as rewards for good behavior.

The best thing to do about toys and play materials would seem to be to give them to the child with no conditions attached, just because they are good for him and stimulate his development. If you make them contingent upon his behavior, you're going to get it right back from him eventually. At moments when he feels unwanted or unloved he's going to want to accumulate things. He'll say, buy me this or buy me that. That becomes his way of saying he feels unloved. But if he doesn't associate those things with being loved, he's not likely to use them that way. Instead he'll come to you and say, "You don't love me"—or maybe draw a picture of his family without you in it. Then you can ask him why he feels that way and come to grips with the situation directly.

Just as the infant's play with parts of his body leads into play with soft toys, which leads to play with other kinds of toys he can manipulate and eventually learn to use in order to produce certain effects, so nursery school and kindergarten lead from this kind of manipulative play with objects to the development of various skills that require perceptive judgment and patient effort. In this way play eventually becomes work. What a young child has to learn from his play, in the process of building with blocks or painting a picture or putting all the clothespins in the bottle or fitting all the pieces into the puzzle, is to be able, for the sake of some finished product, to control his desire to destroy, break or mess things. He has to learn to plan ahead and to tolerate frustration for some anticipated goal.

11

Setting Limits

PUNISHMENT AND DISCIPLINE are two different things. Discipline involves a discernible pattern, a structure within which the child can function with a sense of predictability. This is a very important aspect of his life. All of us, when we don't know what is going to happen to us, feel overwhelmed or anxious. All human beings have a need to be able to predict what they will experience to some extent, in order to prepare themselves to adjust to it. If we feel we know pretty much what is likely to happen in our lives we feel less anxiety and a greater degree of security.

Children who are exposed to an inconsistent environment, where limits are ambiguously stated or where they have no way of knowing what will happen as a result of what they do, are very anxious children and often very destructive ones. They are destructive not because of aggressive instincts but because they are asking somebody to stop them.

Certain species of animals go to the fringes of their territory and make challenging faces at the animals in the adjacent area in order to establish who belongs where, so everyone will know his own place. In a similar way, the child who misbehaves is sometimes asking you to say, "No, you can't do that." Children feel safer and are more productive in a structured environment; this has been demonstrated by research and confirmed by clinical experience. An atmosphere of complete freedom seems to lead to feelings of insecurity and various kinds of provocative "testing" behavior. "Problem" children have been found to be much more productive in an environment that is structured but offers them some gradually increasing freedom within that structure. Sometimes when you see destructive behavior in your children, it may mean that the limits you had previously set are wearing rather thin —and it's time to reaffirm what they are.

Some parents, when they find their patience beginning to wear thin, give a child fair warning by means of a kind of countdown. "If you aren't in bed by the time I count five . . ." The enterprising son of one man we know asked one evening, "Dad, could you make it six?" which his father was happy to do. This was the young man's attempt to maintain some participation in his fate—to influence the outcome of events in his life.

Sometimes mothers and fathers think they ought to give children an explanation for every instruction. This isn't really necessary or even appropriate at this age. You needn't reason with a toddler; he won't understand any but the simplest explanations anyway, and you'll probably only confuse him with the *why*. This can make him feel anxious and lead him to engage in a good deal of provocative behavior to test out the limits that seem so confusing. You can reason with him later, when he's older. Now it's perfectly all right just to say a firm "no" to certain things. He needs to learn what the rules are, and that you're going to enforce them in a firm but friendly way. Philosophy can come later.

We have to distinguish here between the kinds of explanations we give a child in order to prepare him for something new or unexpected that is going to happen to him—going to the hospital, for instance, or starting nursery school, or taking a plane trip—and giving him exhaustive explanations of your reasons for everything you want him to do. One little boy of four whose mother was painstakingly explaining why she wanted him to put on his rubbers burst out, "I'll wear them if you don't tell me why I have to."

What about spanking?

There is probably nothing wrong with spanking children provided you give them adequate warning and don't really hurt them. Sometimes you have to say to a child, "If you do that once more, I'm going to spank you." And if he does do it again, you have to spank him. You don't have to hurt him, but you do have to spank him. Eventually, he learns that you mean what you say. If you do spank him, you can point out that you don't really want to treat him this way but he really gives you no other choice if he does not respond to what you tell him. You're really giving the child a certain freedom, rather than making him feel powerless and uncertain. You're saying, "Be naughty if you insist, but this will be the consequence." You're giving him the choice; he can determine whether he'll get the spanking or not. However, if you haul off and hit him without any warning, that's a different story. That's not discipline, it's punishment. And punishment only teaches him to be wary of getting caught.

There are many times, though, when you can forestall an eyeball-to-eyeball confrontation, times when you can see what your child is about to do and prevent the situation by distracting him. This is often a more constructive solution, since the tendency to behave in the way that's at issue may simply disappear with time as he grows beyond a particular stage of childhood.

The two-year-old who won't allow you to dress him so you can go to the park can sometimes be distracted with a picture book to look at while you stuff him into his snowsuit. If all else fails and you decide to discipline him by some consequence, it's a good idea to make sure that the consequence is related to the behavior itself. For instance, if you decide to withhold television the following day, you're going to be doing two things. First of all, you're making television very important, more important than it should be. And secondly, you're projecting the consequence so far ahead that it has no meaning for the child now. This might be the time to take a firm stand, to say, "We're going out to the park. Now if I have to hold you down and dress you like a tiny little baby I'm going to do it."

Sometimes you not only have to be firm but strong too. Remember, you're a grownup and he's a little child, and if he is to understand reality and feel secure in the world you must help him to acknowledge that there's a big difference between children and grownups. When you put yourself on the child's level, communication breaks down; but when in effect you say, "Look, I'm the mother—or the father—and this is what you have to do," as long as you're not mean about it, even though the child may not seem to respond positively at the time, you are getting across the idea that this is a consistent, stable universe and one it's possible to learn to function in because there are some definite rules.

The moment you have to bargain on any terms with a child, you're in trouble. Probably the best idea is to use your own feelings as the only currency with which to negotiate. He learns that you're happy with him when he does this, and unhappy with him when he does that, that you get irritated with him sometimes, or even so annoyed that you don't want to play with him. He'll want to please you if he enjoys your attentions.

A child who feels the need for more attention may be telling you this when he misbehaves. He may welcome a scene or a spanking. Negative attention is, after all, better than no attention to a child. And he may make trouble as a means of getting his parents to pay some attention to him.

Teaching children social behavior is a way of helping them learn to adapt themselves to the real world. As a matter of fact, we continue testing the limits of reality throughout our lives to see how far we can go. Children will continue to test you as part of the process of learning about their environment, a way of finding out what the world will and will not allow. If the limits become inconsistent—if you allow something to be tolerated now but not at some other time—a child is made uncomfortable by his uncertainty regarding the future consequences of his behavior, and will have a much greater tendency to challenge you as a way of finding out.

If you're very punitive, a child isn't likely to respond to your values unless you're there. Like that dog who jumps off the couch every time you enter the room, he won't have learned not to do certain things; he'll have learned that when you're around he shouldn't do them. The dog has not internalized the idea that it's bad to sit on couches; he has merely attached the idea to you. He associates you with punishment for sitting on the couch.

Children behave in a similar way with parents. If you're harshly punitive, what the child learns is that you're a scary person; he won't do the things he knows you object to as long as you're there, but when you're not there, he will do them.

If, on the other hand, you're generally firm and consistent about the rules and the child thinks of you as a fair person and has learned to trust and depend on you, your rules and values become internalized, part of the child himself, so that you don't always have to be there for him to behave. His own conscience will not only operate when you're there but will take over when you're not there.

Most children want someone to set firm limits. It matters less what exactly your limits are than that you be consistent about them. The degree to which you're ambiguous is directly proportional to the degree to which the child may try to manipulate you into taking a firm stand, constantly testing the limits. Often a child tries to find out if there's anybody around who's strong enough to provide him with consistency so he can relax and say, "Okay, now I know what the rules are."

One of the disadvantages of having many people take care of your child is that often they have different expectations from yours with regard to the child's behavior. While an older child may benefit from learning to respond to various people and situations in numerous ways, a young child who is just learning to do things for himself will have to shift gears when different people take over the function of showing him how, whether by words or example. This is not to say you shouldn't leave a child with a maid, a friend or a relative sometimes, but you should try to ensure a certain consistency for the child by making sure it's not a succession of different maids, friends, or relatives, and that those who do take care of him do things in pretty much the same way you do and expect the same things from him.

There are some parents who believe in not creating any frustration for their children at all. They think they should have complete freedom in expressing themselves and feel that any inhibition of this freedom would in some way hold the child back. This is nonsense, and such mothers and fathers are not providing experience of value for their young children—they are failing to give them something very important to their future.

The best time to teach a child how society expects him to behave is when he is ready to learn it. There is a point at which the child is receptive to and gets a sense of satisfaction out of mastering certain things, and if you don't help him learn how to master some of his desires and impulses at this point he isn't going to be prepared for the next stage in his developmnt, when he will need to use this control.

A good parent helps a child learn how to cope with reality and how to master his impulses in relation to the demands of society. He or she is not a parent who pushes, not a parent who overprotects, who always does things *for* the child. If you go on doing things for him, you don't help the child learn to do them for himself. On the other hand, if you make demands a child is not ready to meet, you're putting him under pressure to which he may not be able to respond.

If we had to take one definition and say "This is what a good parent is," we would say it's the one who equips a child to deal with as many of the kinds of situations that come up in life as possible. If you go on allowing a child to do whatever he wants to—whether it's eating with his fingers instead of a fork, or taking other children's shovels in the sandbox—because you don't want to frustrate him, eventually he's going to run into problems he's not equipped to handle.

There are some very good reasons for teaching toddlers manners. Aren't you more comfortable when your child says "please" and "thank you"? So are other people, and he has the gratifying experience of pleasing other people, an important factor in his social development. Children who, without losing the quality of being a child, show respect for other people and for things in their environment, and who don't infringe on other people's rights, are much more accepted. People are glad to have them around.

This doesn't mean you shouldn't allow your child to smear with finger paint, to run around in the park, to splash up the bathroom once in a while. But the important thing is to balance freedom with control. Parents who only think about their children's being neat and clean and polite restrict them in such a way that they haven't enough kinds of experience to learn from, while the "non-frustration" parents bring up children who have no limits and just don't seem to get socialized. Eventually, not too many people will want those children around.

When they grow up, they can't plan for the future, they can't accept the limitations that other people do on their social behavior. Many of the people who come to psychotherapy from overpermissive homes and schools are at a loss because their kind of environment did not provide them with the capacity to plan for the future. They were allowed to express all their urges, do anything they wanted to do "right now," without paying any attention to long-range consequences.

As parents, our obligation is not just to make our children happy for the moment so they will love us and make *us* feel good, but to help them learn to forego the immediate pleasure of doing what they want to do at the moment on occasions when it's necessary in order to achieve gratification at some time in the future.

12

Feeding and the Training Process

IN EVERY ASPECT of his behavior, the helpless and dependent baby of the first months of life is gradually moving toward mastery of his own body, control of the environment and mature relationships with others.

You can see this process taking place quite clearly in the area of feeding. By the last part of his first year the baby will begin learning to feed himself. Like all developmental processes, it's a now-and-then affair, a touch-and-go business at best. Sometimes a baby who's been happily drinking from a cup will want his bottle back again. And the mechanics of moving little bits of meat or vegetables from his plate to his mouth won't go smoothly until after much trial and error and a good deal of decoration of the floor and furniture.

This is the way things are—something to expect rather than to worry about. Occasional regression back to an earlier level is as much a part of every child's development as progress is, and every child grows in somewhat the same manner as the legendary frog who took one step backward for every three he took forward. Development never proceeds smoothly in a straight line but back and forth over a long period of time, and in the early years babies will have alternating periods of happily drinking from a cup and eating with a spoon and then wanting their bottles back again, just as they will occasionally return to babbling after learning to speak words, will sometimes soil themselves after learning to use the toilet, or play with their own bodies instead of the toys they've begun to show an interest in. All is not lost because these things happen, and wise parents simply encourage the progress without making too much fuss about the occasional regression. It's not easy to learn so many new jobs at once, as any grownup who's tried to learn even one new job at a time will realize. And making too much fuss about his occasional lapses gives them a kind of premium attention value which may even encourage him to do the same thing again. It's usually better to offer positive encouragement and approval as a reward for learning something new rather than focusing a lot of negative attention on the old way.

Throughout infancy, mealtimes continue to be the main area of interaction between mother and child, even as he takes on more of the actual feeding task himself. He still associates food with mother, and how he reacts to new feeding experiences reflects this. A baby whose needs have been gratified in the early months by a responsive mother to whom he has a strong and mutually satisfying attachment will, as we have said before, feel a sense of trust in the world and confidence in others. He will meet the new tastes and consistencies offered to him with an overall attitude of interest and a willingness to try new things, although of course he can't be expected to like all of them. On the whole, the way he reacts to the introduction of new foods will correspond to the way he responds to change and newness in other areas of his development—either adventurous or clinging to the old ways and feeling all change is threatening. However, this is a general pattern we are describing. No baby, as we have said, proceeds in a straight unbroken line in any area of his development, and there may be not only occasional regressions but also other kinds of behavior that are common through transient problems.

Many babies seem to develop a craving for sweets as a substitute for the sucking pleasure they relinquish when they give up the bottle for the cup. A balanced diet has to be considered from a certain perspective in time. Some babies have days of preferring cookies to anything else and then want nothing but meat for a while; others crave milk to the exclusion of any other liquid and then suddenly switch to pineapple juice, but if you consider their diet over a period of a month or so, studies have shown their natural tastes usually result in a well-balanced diet. So there's no reason to be unduly worried about indulging a baby's taste for cookies—or pretzels, or bananas, or mustard for that matter—at a time when it may be due to some psychological association you're not aware of. A baby's diet will usually balance out in the long run if his tastes are not warped by parental pressure or mealtime battles. And it's a good principle to follow that he can't be expected to give anything up that has been important to him without finding something else to take its place.

Food fads arise very often during the time a child is being toilet trained. He sees your displeasure if he soils himself or messes in his bed, and in identifying with your reaction, some of the disgust he is learning to feel may spill over into the area of foods and he may absolutely refuse to touch mashed potatoes, asparagus or even birthday cake. This behavior is common at this stage of development.

It's generally true that if you make him happy, a baby

wants to grow. He wants to give up all that dependency. He doesn't want things like a breast or a bottle holding him back. He has an urge to get around and explore his environment, and when he does, it's time to set realistic limits and begin to socialize him—sometime around the end of his first year. Around the middle of his second year you can begin to show him how you use a fork and spoon and how you shake hands with people and when to say please and thank you. At this point he will want to imitate everything you do, and this is the time to get across some kinds of cultural behavior.

Some time between two and three most children are ready for toilet training. If you start them much earlier than the age of two you don't accomplish toilet training. You may condition them to some schedule which is convenient for you, but it's not training. They do not yet have the capacity to control their sphincter muscles and can't really stop urination or defecation once it begins.

Children are all different, just as all mothers are different. They have different degrees of readiness, just as mothers have different degrees of intuition. A child will usually show an interest in using the toilet once he is physically ready and you've given him the opportunity by showing him what it's for and explaining that this is what people do—that to be like Mommy or Daddy or his sisters or brothers, when he feels he has to go he should come and sit on the toilet. This is a necessary part of the process because there is no instinct that tells a child what a toilet is for. Training will be imitative, because from about a year and a half to three years or so, children want to do almost everything they see you do out of a desire to be like you, to be one with you. This is a developmental process which can be made good use of to encourage training at the right time. Pushing it before he is physically ready or has any desire to learn and setting up a resistance on his part can turn what should be a gradual natural process into a battle of wills. In that kind of battle, no one wins.

Why make a battleground of toilet training anyway? Why force him into certain behavior patterns when you can, with some patience, take advantage of his tendency to want to do certain things your way because he identifies with you and wants to please you and be like you? Remember that once a battle has been pitched, he is bound to lose—in the long run. Confrontations of this kind go against the developmental needs of this period. They make him feel overpowered, weak and ashamed of himself at a time when he should begin to feel capable of setting a direction and acting for himself to some extent.

For this reason, it's well worth waiting until he is biologically ready, so he can control himself and have the feeling training is voluntary, not something he is being subjected to and overpowered by. A gradual on-and-off process is the natural course of development in all things.

It's a good idea to try not to do anything in such a way as to make him feel he is not the one who is in control of his own bodily functions. At this age, he needs to begin to have a sense of this kind of self-mastery.

Let's look at toilet training for a moment from the child's point of view. The grownups are asking him to do a certain thing at a certain time in a certain place and in a certain way, for which he receives some degree of increased positive or negative attention. If a parent becomes excited or deliriously happy with how much, where, when and how the child performs, the child may very well conclude that his bodily products are extremely important as a means of getting attention and satisfaction.

Can you imagine how he will then feel when what he's produced is flushed down the toilet, after such a fuss has been made about its importance?

It's as unrealistic for parents to overreact in a positive way to the child's performance as it is to become punitive and demanding, to threaten punishment unless he gives up what they seem to want from him in a specified way.

We know that children this age think in magical terms. They believe something may happen because they thought it, just as they think that totally unrelated things may cause each other. Preschool children think the snake they imagine in the closet really exists, or that you come into the room because they cross their fingers three times. One little boy was convinced he had caused the blackout of the entire East Coast in 1965 because he had been tapping on a lamp he had been told not to touch at the moment when the blackout occurred. By the same token, the young child may fear that something bad will happen if he fails to carry out some particular ritual. Christopher Robin's image of "the masses of bears/ Who wait at the corners all ready to eat/ The sillies who tread on the lines of the street" is a universal kind of thought among children.

A child's fear of angering a parent who is easily upset by lapses in the toilet ritual may lead to an undue concern with neatness, orderliness and cleanliness, and may cause a child to engage in ritualistic behavior as a means of warding off parental anger. Eventually this kind of behavior is generalized into warding off all kinds of dangers, and a child may develop compulsive patterns of behavior, things he must do in a certain way at a certain time. If he does not, he feels extremely uncomfortable. Some have a compulsion to wash their hands frequently, some to dress in a certain ritualistic way, some to touch every telephone pole they pass or chew each mouthful of food a certain number of times, but whatever the particular pattern, behind it is the fear that if they do not follow it something terrible will happen. Clinically, we can see how this kind of behavior sometimes develops out of an undue concern with cleanliness, neatness and order related to harsh or punitive early toilet training.

What we think we are teaching is not always what the child is learning. A parent may think he is teaching toilet training while what a child is really learning is to perform tasks in a certain kind of way in order to avoid having to face a parent's dissatisfaction and anger. At this age a child has an intense fear of separation from his parents, physical or emotional. The child is in conflict about whether to do what he wants to or give in passively to his parents' demands. When a child resists toilet training or lapses once in a while, it may be part of the process of his learning to cope with his own wishes at the same time that he complies with those of his parents. He needs to know he can express some of his own impulses—once in a while, even "naughty" ones—without its meaning complete disaster. The violence of some parents' anger, or their inability to forgive and forget, can seem like the end of the world to a small child, and he may become overly passive or obsessional, unable to make the slightest decision for himself, out of an exaggerated fear of making the wrong decision and the early-founded feeling that if he does, it will bring on disaster. He may no longer remember either the force or the tenacity of his parents' wrath, but its effects may continue to influence his behavior in later life.

An important principle in this phase of childhood is to avoid overemphasizing and distorting the meaning and importance of toilet training. It's important for the child to feel he can get off the potty or training seat, not to be strapped on and made to feel coerced. And he shouldn't be threatened or punished if he balks at the whole idea sometimes.

He may sit on the toilet for half an hour without doing anything and then defecate as soon as you've put him into a clean diaper. The best thing to do in the face of the child's reluctance is probably to continue to encourage his efforts and think in terms of positive ways of helping him (Is he afraid of the toilet? Would he be more comfortable on a potty chair where he could have his feet on the ground?), rather than concentrating a lot of negative attention on his balkiness. Making too much of a fuss may do more harm than good. He'll learn eventually if you are patient and consistent. Forcing him into a certain pattern of behavior may mean a couple of months less of inconvenience for you now but years of trouble later on.

A young child is likely to be frightened if the toilet is flushed while he is sitting on it, and even after he gets off he may want to keep what he's made there instead of flushing it away. He may want to look at it, even say "bye-bye." Children this age do not clearly differentiate their own bodies from the products of their own bodies. We see this same phenomenon in primitive cultures in which people hide or bury or burn remnants of themselves, such as hair or fingernails, so no enemy will find them or no sorcerer gain power over them.

Not every child responds the same way to the same experience. An overemphasis on the accomplishment of toilet training sometimes leads to an obsessive-compulsive character disorder, sometimes to its very opposite, a person who is aggressively sloppy and dirty. Both extremes —rebellious messiness and passive overneatness—are patterns of behavior which can influence an individual's adjustment to adult life either in terms of the work he does or his relationships with other people.

13

Learning to Live with Others

SOMETIME TOWARD THE END of their first year most babies begin to differentiate between the people they see. They often show a new fear of strangers. A baby who at six months smiled and gurgled at anyone who smiled and talked to him may very well at nine months turn his face away and begin to cry bitterly at the approach of any person he does not know well. He may begin to cling to his mother when other people are around and set up a howl whenever she leaves him.

Some parents worry that this is a sign that something is wrong, but actually this behavior is a normal development in a healthy baby of this age and a sign that something is just as it should be—the baby has established a close tie to his mother. This attachment is based on his experience that she gratifies his needs and comforts him when he's distressed, and such a positive attachment to a mothering figure seems to be a necessary precursor of the ability to relate positively to other people later in life.

In addition, the baby's perceptual apparatus has developed to the point where he is able to perceive not only the difference between his mother and other people, but between the various other people themselves. He may associate different individuals with things we are not aware of—a loud voice that frightens him, a fondness for tickling that irritates him, an odor of cigar smoke he doesn't like—and the result can sometimes be embarrassing for his poor parents, as when he cries every time a particular uncle comes near him.

It's the baby to whom it doesn't matter *who* takes care of him who may be in trouble. A baby who shows absolutely no differentiation in his response to different people isn't really reacting to other people at all, as is often the case with babies in institutions.

In his first year the baby really learns one important thing—either to trust the world or to mistrust it. A baby who is frustrated, who is not picked up when he needs to be, is not fed when he needs to be, begins to feel that the whole world cannot be trusted to satisfy his needs. But if he acquires a feeling of confident expectation in that first year, then in the second year you can begin to set limits and exert discipline. He will want to please those for whom he has formed strong positive feelings.

From the developmental point of view then, the preference for his mother is a healthy sign in a normal baby, and his angry cries when she leaves him, or when someone he doesn't know, however friendly, holds out her arms to take him from his mother, are a sign of strength of his developing personality, a healthy indication that he feels able to register a protest. The resigned baby who seems to feel powerless to influence his environment just accepts whatever comes his way because he doesn't have enough feeling about himself or about others to make the effort seem worthwhile.

One thing parents can do during this phase of intense stranger-anxiety is to keep the baby with them whenever it's not actually inconvenient. This phase will pass, and the baby who feels secure about his parents' love and attention at this stage will find it easier to move away from them when he can walk and run and discover the world beyond them. He feels it's *his* idea to go. The baby who has had constant experiences of being left under protest will cling to his parents for a far longer time. Needing repeated reassurance that they won't abandon him, he is less prone to turn his back on them, since he's in the habit of worrying about where they may disappear to.

If you enjoy it, there's no reason not to keep a baby under a year old with you as much of the time as possible. In addition to the emotional satisfaction of being near their parents, babies who are taken places with them are receiving a much greater amount of stimulation than those who are left at home.

And you needn't worry unduly about "exposing them to germs." There is some evidence for the value of exposing infants to the environment. Babies who are kept under ultrasanitary conditions seem to become ill more easily later on because their bodies don't learn to fight off infection. At the same time, if they see a lot of people, and observe different kinds of behavior, they learn there are many kinds of people in the world, and they're not as fearful of strangers later on. Children who are kept in a very restricted environment are more easily overwhelmed by newness and change, and one important aspect of emotional development is the capacity to adapt to change.

There are bound to be *some* occasions on which you'll have to leave him home, though, and a good thing to do when you're going out is to have the person with whom you're going to leave the baby come in before he goes to sleep. If the baby sees the sitter and you at the same time, before you go out, it's easier for him to establish a connection, to make the transition from the sitter to you, than if he wakes up and suddenly finds there's somebody else there when he expected his mother. A young baby has no understanding of time, no concept of contingency, and may very well have the feeling he's been abandoned by her forever.

A child who has established a close tie with his mother in the first year or two usually will begin to explore other things when she is present. When he is in a new place or with new people, very often he will look back to make sure his mother is there. He will come running or crawling back just for a reassuring touch or to be picked up for a moment. Then she can put him down and he will go off to explore again. Little children are very much aware of the fact that they're dependent upon that one person who understands their needs and who will come when they cry, feed them when they're hungry, pick them up when they need comfort, and change them when they're wet. If they don't feel that way they're not inclined to come to one person—almost anyone will do. All the evidence we have suggests that in order to be able to establish a close, deep relationship with another person when they grow up, it is very important for children to establish a close tie with one person when they're little. It becomes a point of embarkation into other relationships with other people.

For his first few years, until he goes to school, the all-important people in the child's life are those in his immediate family. What meaning does a new baby in the family have for a very young child?

The birth of a second baby can be very difficult for the first, who's been an only child up to now. In a sense, it represents a tragedy in a child's life. That may seem like a very strong word, but little children do react very intensely. When they cry, they scream; when they're angry, they destroy; and when they feel you're not there, their grief is the equivalent of what we feel when someone close to us dies—they feel they've lost you forever.

Think what a young child must feel when all of a sudden the family is no longer three but four, and he sees someone else getting the affection and attention that were all his when he was the only child. He can't help sometimes wishing things could be the way they were before. Then, of course, he may feel guilty about it. A very young child may even think you'll be able to read his thoughts and might stop loving him because of them. Then he'll kiss and hug the baby and bend over backward to be attentive, not out of love but as a kind of defense against his own guilt. Sometimes, just when older children are showing a new baby the most love, it's at least partly because they're jealous and this is their way of coping with the feeling. Actually, it's a pretty constructive way! If you're aware of their feelings you can give them a little extra attention of their own and at the same time praise them for helping with the baby, thus meeting their need and reinforcing their socially desirable behavior at the same time.

A small child whose world has been invaded by a sister or brother is bound to have at least a few negative reactions. Children have different ways of manifesting their feelings in this situation, as in all things. Some try to act like babies themselves, as though they think if they start drinking from bottles again or go back to wetting their diapers, *they* will be the center of attention again instead of the newcomer. Others become extra good, as though they think that if they don't watch their step they'll be out, entirely replaced by the usurper. Still others become openly aggressive, and may even try to hurt the baby in more or less subtle ways, as though they think if they could get rid of him everything would be the way it was before.

In handling this situation, it's a good idea not to make the child feel that he is bad, to let him know that you love him as much as ever and at the same time that you are firmly in control of the situation and will not let him hurt the baby—or anyone else, including himself. He'll be reassured to know he's safe from his own dangerous impulses and conclude that you'll protect him in the same way that you do the baby.

Too many self-conscious verbal expressions of love don't really help the older child faced with a new baby in the family. He may very well reason there must be something wrong, or else why all the fuss? This is a time when actions can speak louder than words—finding time to be with him, for one thing. If he is alone with you and you seem to be enjoying his company—whether you're taking him for a walk, baking a cake or doing the week's marketing—he won't need to be told you still love him. And if you don't seem to have time for him any more, no amount of verbal reassurance is going to convince him.

It's one of the distinguishing features of our increasingly competitive society that an individual's success is usually seen to imply some other person's failure. A healthier situation would be the ability to look at another's success as reflecting on the whole group, and a good way to encourage such an outlook would be to begin in the home, in the family situation that involves the feelings of brothers and sisters toward each other in relation to their parents' love. Parents should try to avoid stimulating any more competition between their children than is inevitable. Every parent will find the ways that work best in his or her particular family. A few general suggestions may help give the idea. Try not to take time away from one child to spend with another, or let it work out that the one who screams or fusses the most gets the most attention, but have some time that really belongs to each child and cannot be taken away, whether it's time spent looking at a picture book, going to the park or doing something together around the house. Seeing that you always have a certain time to be with him and listen to him means more than anything you can possibly say about still loving him as much as you did before the baby came.

It's doubtful whether any useful purpose is served by the habit of making comparisons of your child with other children. The parent who is always pointing to a classmate, a cousin or a neighbor's child as an example of model behavior only stimulates resentment and the most sterile kind of competitiveness—the desire for praise rather than for achievement for its own sake. A child should help with the dishes because it's what you expect of her, not because your friend's daughter does it. Don't compare your child with other children unless you're prepared for him to compare you with other parents in the same way.

There is probably no way to do away entirely with some degree of rivalry between brothers and sisters, each of whom would really like to have all of his parents' love and attention, but it's possible to minimize it. One way is by treating the children in a family as individuals, rather than always trying to equate things for them. Some parents think they have to give each of their children the same things all the time. If one child gets a particular toy, they have to get the same thing for their other child. But life won't always offer any two people the same things, and to create such expectations is not really helping them to adapt to the reality they'll have to face and deal with when they leave the family circle someday.

If you always try to equate things for them, you're liable to find them doing things because "he does it" or wanting things because "she has it." This only increases the rivalry.

You can help them to realize their differences as individuals and respond to their particular needs, starting right off when they're very young with the differences in their age—and, when it applies, in their sex. You can point out when they complain that *she* has or does this or that, that she's a girl, or she's *herself,* and a different kind of person from you. "This is what *she* likes. What do *you* like?" Even if the child comes right back with "I like the same thing!" you're introducing the idea that they are two distinct individuals and can be expected to have different tastes and reactions. You can help them to realize their differences by responding to their particular needs in different ways.

If you can involve an older child in helping you take care of a new baby without making it a burden for him, you can give him a realistically based sense of his own importance to you and help him channel some of his natural destructive tendencies.

Children's play gives dramatic evidence of their feelings, conscious or unconscious, toward their little brothers and sisters. In their games and in their fantasies they often dispose of the interlopers quite directly—in the garbage can ("*and* put the lid on," went the litany of one three-year-old), down the incinerator or out the window. You are helping them in a very important way if you lead them to find socially acceptable ways of dealing with these feelings. If they learn to cope with these tensions and get rid of the hostility and competitiveness they feel in play and games, this is an ability they can make use of later on when they find themselves in competitive situations with peers in school and still later in work situations. The child who never learns socially acceptable means of coping with his sibling rivalry is most likely to have problems later on in situations that involve friends (Why wasn't *I* invited to that party?) or working associates (Why didn't *I* get that promotion?). There are people who automatically get into trouble with the people they work side by side with, and very often you can trace this back to early family difficulties of their own. Parents cannot eliminate the problem, but they can try to teach the child helpful ways of coping with it, helping him to verbalize his feelings and divert some of his energy and impulses into building-up-and-knocking-down play with blocks or paints or into competitive games.

PART 3

Toward a Separate Self: The Child Grows Up

14

The Nursery Years: A World Beyond Mother

WHEN WE TALKED about the behavior of the human being in the first months of life we had to say much more about his physiology than we do now that he is older. At first, most of his behavior was instinctive and he had to be considered primarily as a physical organism. The infant cannot exist without someone who mothers him—who feeds him and protects him, keeps him warm and comfortable and provides him with environmental stimulation, holding him, picking him up and carrying him around.

Gradually, as he gets older, he becomes less dependent on that mothering figure. He begins to move around on his own, returning for an occasional glimpse or a touch to reassure himself that she is still there. Little by little he begins to develop a symbolic representation of her. He is getting the idea that she continues to exist even when he does not see her, and that she will still be there when he returns.

At the same time, he is also becoming less of a creature of instinct. His behavior is less biologically determined; we can begin to talk about a relatively separate psychological aspect of his behavior. He has learned from his early experiences, been shaped by his environment. Social and cultural forces have already had an influence on what he is like and on what he has learned.

His mental processes are making the transition from images and magical connections to thinking in logical relationships. It will be some time before he understands causal connections or abstract concepts like time, but he is beginning to ask why things happen and how, what things are and where they go when he no longer sees them.

Now the child is no longer an infant, but a preschooler. From about three to five he becomes able to leave his mother for short periods of time and venture out into the world. Nursery school and kindergarten usually represent the transition from babyhood to the relatively greater independence of his school years.

The child's main task is learning to be independent, and emotional disorders in these years may take the form of a need to cling to his parents or of exaggerated fears and phobias, which fix him at a level of dependency that interferes with his moving on in psychological and social growth. Regressive, clinging behavior and excessive fears often represent the child's inability to cope with some unacceptable impulse toward the person on whom he is dependent. Let's look at the child of this age and see how this is so—how parental attitudes influence the child's development of independence and affect the possibility of preventing emotional disorders.

In early infancy the perceptual apparatus was activated in response to stimulation from the environment. His cognitive development proceeded through his second year or so in the baby's play. He manipulated objects at first through the random exercise of his own body, then observing the effects of his actions on the environment, and later making the connection and purposely acting in order to bring about certain effects. He began by kicking for its own sake, his kicking caused the crib to rattle, and eventually he kicked in order to produce that rattling sound. The basis for his first learning of cause-and-effect relationships was his own exercise of his motor functions.

By the time he is six or seven years old he goes off to a world quite separate from home, a world of books and homework assignments in which he has to learn things he will use in his eventual occupation. He has developed the mental capacity to handle abstract concepts and manipulate symbols, to read and write and deal with number relationships and with ideas of time and place.

Before he reaches that point, though, in the years from about three to six, he needs to learn to master certain more basic skills—focusing his attention, observing distinctive characteristics of things, comparing and relating them. He also has to prepare for the greater independence of the school years during this transitional period by beginning to learn how to cope with the environment in the absence of his mother.

The problems which are so common in so many children during this period of transition between babyhood and childhood—fear of the dark, holding on to mother and reluctance to go off and play with other children—are often determined by the attitudes of parents and by their own earlier experiences.

Take the first day of school. Your own experience on your first day of kindergarten can very directly affect your attitude toward your child in the same situation and how he will then react to that situation in his turn. If you remember your own first day of school as frightening, if you felt very small climbing the huge steps into that forbidding building where you had to let go of your mother's hand and go forward into the unknown all alone, you may naturally enough, even unthinkingly, expect your child to feel the same way when he goes off to nursery school. You may tend to make him feel your own negative outlook, revive your own old fears in him, by means of overelaborate reassurances that he will be all right, that there is nothing to be afraid of, that you will be there when he comes out, that the teacher is really a nice person. What, he may begin to wonder, are all the reassurances for if there is nothing to be reassured about? Maybe you *aren't* going to be there when he comes out! What's all the fuss if there's nothing to be afraid of?

Usually when parents behave this way they are entirely well meaning, and may be totally unaware of the source of their own solicitousness in their own memories. It might be a good idea in helping your child face all new experiences in his life to think a little about what your own feelings are about your similar experiences as you remember them. We don't think parents should ever try to "analyze" or "treat" their own children, probing or interpreting their thoughts, even when they are professional psychologists or psychiatrists. The requirements of the doctor-patient relationship and of the parent-child relationship are quite different. But there's no harm and may even be a lot of good, in using insight on yourself to understand your own behavior toward your children as a reflection of your own needs, so that it doesn't interfere with what you consciously know to be *their* needs at the time. Recalling how you felt on *your* first day of school, for example, can heighten your awareness of your own attitude and help prevent you from imposing on your child either exactly the same or a completely opposite experience.

Probably the most useful way for a parent to react to all new experience on the child's part is matter-of-factly, being honest in appraising the situation and expressing confidence in his capacity to handle it. You only prepare him for failure with constant admonitions that there is nothing to worry about; in a way, you are programing the possibility of failure into his consciousness. It's much better to tell him on the first day of school or when he has to go to the hospital that most children feel a little sad at times like these but that they get over it, and you know he will too. Whether he worries or not will be determined less by your telling him not to worry than by his seeing that you don't seem to be worried yourself. A parent's confidence in his child's ability is a very important factor in his successful performance.

When you overstress the positive implications ("It won't hurt a bit") you leave him to imply the negative ones—and he will. Why not do it the other way around? Let him learn that you'll tell him the worst, and spare him the anxiety in which he has to conjure it up for himself, probably in far worse terms than the reality. Tell him, yes, it will hurt for a moment, letting him see that you have confidence in his ability to handle both the information and the hurt. The implication is that you think he can deal with the experience, and if you treat him as though your expectation is that he *can* cope, he probably will live up to that expectation. It is the child who is insecure about his own abilities who grows into the adolescent with a feeling that nobody has faith in him and who does wild or dangerous things in order to prove his capacities to himself and others.

It's wise to prepare a young child for any kind of change in his life—starting nursery school, taking a trip, the birth of a sibling, a short separation from his parents —or for anything he hasn't done before or that may frighten him. It's a good idea, for instance, before a visit to the doctor, to give him an idea of what to expect there. Telling him about it, even if he doesn't seem to understand all the details at the time, will get the idea across to him that someone he trusts can generally be counted on to prepare him in advance for what is going to happen to him. This can spare him a lot of undue anxiety. He can turn his attention to the many tasks of living, playing and learning without having to worry about the unknown and the unexpected.

In the case of hospitalization, it's especially important to give the child whatever amount of truthful information he is old enough to understand. He is bound to be frightened by the separation from his parents and the strange surroundings in addition to the pain of illness and of whatever medical or surgical procedures he has to undergo. Two things can help him. For the child too young to understand why he is in the hospital, the presence of his mother can make the difference between being able to adjust to the strange people and surroundings, the frightening examinations and operative procedures, or feeling a terror at his abandonment to all this which often leaves permanent emotional scars. Often, when babies and young children left in the hospital stop crying, it's not because they've "settled down" or adjusted to the situation. They have given up, and their despair has all the clinical characteristics of severe depression.

Besides choosing a hospital that encourages mothers to stay with their children for as much of the time they are hospitalized as possible, parents can help a child who is old enough for verbal explanations by giving him an idea of what to expect, letting him ask questions about it, and answering them truthfully, in as much detail as seems appropriate to his age. While a ten-year-old may take a great interest in knowing what an appendix is and how the surgeon will proceed in repairing his, all a three-year-old needs to know is that something inside—where it hurts him—is not working properly and the doctors and nurses are going to fix it for him so it won't hurt any more. A younger child won't even understand this much, and the only possible reassurance for him is the familiar presence of a comforting mother.

One little girl we know was five years old when she was hospitalized for a tonsillectomy. Her parents explained that removing her tonsils would end the infections that had caused her so many earaches, and told her what to expect when she got to the hospital—how she would be admitted, what the ward would look like, that she would be given medicine to put her to sleep before she was taken to the operating room, and that when she woke up her throat would be sore but her mother would be there and would be able to stay with her until it was time to go home the next day.

Her parents prepared her as well as they could, answering her questions and telling her about other children who had had tonsillectomies, reading her a book called *Johnny Goes to the Hospital* and encouraging her to play hospital with her dolls. She wasn't exactly eager when the day came to go to the hospital, but after all, it wasn't a birthday party, and neither did she seem unduly worried. She held their hands and seemed confident that things would be no worse than they had told her they would be. All was well until shortly before time for the operation, when the anesthesiologist, for whom she had been prepared, arrived and introduced himself as a magician, for whom she was *not* prepared, and told her he was about to put her into a magic sleep so he could take her off to the land of the fairies. The little girl began to cry in real fear, then to struggle against being given the medication, and finally she had to be held down and forcibly subjected to procedures she had been prepared to accept voluntarily. She knew the story about magic and fairies wasn't true—it wasn't what she had been told by her parents and besides, she knew there was no such thing. Why would anyone lie

167

to her unless something terrible was going to happen? And who wants to be taken to a land of fairies anyway, when all you want is to stay with your mother and father?

This is a not uncommon example of how well-meaning people who don't really understand the processes of children's thinking can do harm when they intend to do good. The results in this little girl's case were a fear of falling asleep and a reluctance to leave her mother's side for some time after the operation. Understanding parents and much opportunity to talk about and reenact the hospital experience in play finally helped dispose of the symptoms, but how much easier it would have been—on both child and parents—if it could have been prevented in the first place.

Children are better off being helped to come to grips with the truth—told what to expect, allowed to express their fears and worries about it freely, and reassured that while we understand how they feel we think they'll be able to manage the situation—than being lied to. The lie may make it easier for a grownup to manage a child at the moment, but it may also lead to the child's being overwhelmed by an experience he hasn't been prepared for instead of learning to cope with it, and it may contribute to lifelong feelings of anxiety about what may happen next in a world of people who can't be trusted. Is it worth it?

This child was luckier than many who have similar experiences the effects of which go unrecognized and untreated. Sometimes parents and even hospital personnel take the easy way out for themselves. A child may be easier to handle if we lie to him, if we let him cry until he gives up expecting an answer to his cries, or if he settles into a quiet depression and stops expecting his mother to be at his side. These are the "good" babies and little children who lie quietly staring out of their institutional cribs and beds, and they certainly are easier to manage than children who require explanations, who question, who cry and make demands because they still conceive of the world around them as responding to their needs. But it costs the individual, the family and society a great deal later on to make up for these economies of the moment.

People who don't trust other people are often those who have been lied to as children. They have been taught by their early experience to distrust others.

The question of telling the truth to children often comes up in connection with the popular myths about Santa Claus or the Easter bunny. Many parents feel they don't want to take all the fun and fantasy out of childhood, but are also understandably reluctant to tell their children anything that they know the children will sooner or later recognize to have been lies. How do you enable a little boy to enjoy the sight of Santa Claus even though he sees a different one on every street corner? And how do you save the charm of fantasy for a child in whom you've encouraged enough intelligence to know that reindeer don't go flying through the air or packages arrive via the chimney?

One way is by telling him that there really is no Santa Claus but that everyone sort of pretends there is, thereby saving fun as well as face. This would seem to solve the dilemma of the child's need for fantasy—the pleasure taken in imaginative flights of fancy—and his need for reality—the importance of coming to understand the nature of the real world. You needn't destroy a child's ability to enjoy myths and fairy tales; you can enjoy them with him, as long as you help him to distinguish, as you do, what we are making believe exists from what "really is."

In addition to their interest in fantasy, little children have a great interest in the real world, and especially in themselves. Sex play commonly begins at around three or four and is a natural form of behavior at this age. The child's curiosity about the world starts with his own body and those of other people, big and little. It's common for children this age to play "doctor," to close the door in order to exclude the adults and then inspect each other's bodies.

The healthiest adult attitude toward this behavior is probably not to overreact one way or the other. It's to be expected in children this age and shouldn't either be given undue importance or distorted by parents who let it upset them or who condone it. Both things frighten the child and give his play an emotional meaning which it really doesn't have at this age, when he is primarily concerned with finding out the differences between boys and girls, between children and adults, between himself and others.

It's a good idea to set reasonable limits on this kind of play, not getting angry about it but letting young children know—after they've had a chance to see each other so there's no great mystery left unsolved—that this is not a kind of play that's approved of and then providing other things for them to do. The child in this situation, as always, needs to be given a level of stimulation he can handle at the time, not an overwhelming amount of exposure to nudity or sexual activity that would lead to guilt or fear and withdrawal. Sensible parents usually show mild disapproval—"This is silly," but not "This is bad"— so as to discourage overstimulation in play, but they recognize that the interest in sex is normal at this age and they don't go to pieces over it.

It's probably a good thing if nursery-age boys and girls have some casual opportunity to observe the bodies of other children their own age, either at home or in a shared bathroom at nursery school, when their curiosity is primarily intellectual and less emotionally involved than it will be later. It's usually best not to leave them alone too long in this kind of play situation or to allow it between boys and other boys or girls and other girls, or between children one of whom is much older than the other. One factor is predisposing children to homosexuality or to sexual difficulties of various kinds may be who gets to them first, and it's probably healthiest if the child's first thoughts about sex as well as his first gratifying sexual experience later on take place in a context consistent with reproduction and family life.

This is the time to provide children with the answers and attitudes they will draw on in adolescence when their interest in sex is revived in the context of their newly developing sexual capacities. Their questions about intercourse, conception, pregnancy and birth should be answered honestly to the extent that they ask and on a level that they can understand. They don't have to be told everything at once. They need time to digest new information and then they'll come back and ask again and again. At each stage of development they can be told the same things in a new way, a way they can now understand. How they feel about what you tell them is as important as the information itself, and they will take their cues from your feelings. A few minutes of warm, mutually enjoyable give and take can be worth more than a complete but impersonal lecture.

But openness in talking and explaining and frankness in attitude should not be confused with openness in behavior. Young children should not be exposed to adult sexual activity, particularly their own parents'. Children are aware of more around them than many grownups realize, and when they overhear bedroom scenes or see adults making love, expressions of pleasure may seem to them like pain, and they may interpret what they see or hear as hurting or even suffocating. They are too young to respond to this kind of activity with pleasure themselves, and may not be able to understand that grownups do. This kind of experience can cause deep-rooted sexual fears and contribute to a homosexual solution of later conflicts by predisposing the child to avoid sexual activity with members of the opposite sex, a predisposition which may be reinforced in a vulnerable child later at school or camp.

To a very great extent a child's healthy sexual development depends on identification with the parent of the same sex—with his desire to be like that parent. He should feel a certain degree of respect, and should think of that parent as a gratifying person—not only to him but to the other parent. A boy should be able to identify with a father he clearly sees recognized by his mother as someone who makes her happy and whom she respects. The boy learns how to feel about women from the behavior his father shows toward his mother and parents who show their warmth toward each other in the presence of their children do more to foster healthy sexual attitudes than any books or lectures can do.

There's a positive value in demonstrating one's affection in front of children. Many people who have difficulty showing their affection for those they love feel that it is unacceptable, may even feel guilty about it, partly because they grew up in homes in which they never saw their own parents show love and tenderness toward each other. They never experienced warm contact—an occasional hug, a spontaneous kiss—between their parents or between their parents and themselves as part of everyday life.

There's also no necessary harm in a child's happening to witness occasional family quarrels which are then resolved. He sees that people can have disagreements without destroying their relationship, that it is possible to feel and to express aggression toward someone and still continue to love him. The young child who is rushed out of the way and listens to the sound of angry voices from another room may be more affected by the scene his parents try to hide from him than one who is told frankly that, yes, they quarrel sometimes, but they make up afterward and go on loving each other.

Our expectations of ourselves and of others are greatly influenced by what we experience at home early in life. A parent who can give warmth and comfort to a child, not always words, teaches a child to be tender and to expect tenderness from others. If a child is crying, it may be more effective to produce a tissue, wipe his nose, and put an arm around him, without a word, than to say the most sympathetic things from a distance. It seems to do something special for the young child, for whom the language of the senses still takes precedence over words.

How a child feels about the parent of the same sex determines in large measure how he will feel about his own adult role. No father or mother is perfect; everyone has some weaknesses. The important thing is not for the child to feel the parent is perfect or without weaknesses but that one need not be overwhelmed by them; that imperfections don't necessarily cause loss of self-esteem.

Young children sometimes make attempts to separate their parents. To help them learn to deal with reality, it's generally best to make it perfectly clear to them in a kindly way that they cannot come between their parents. Actually, they are reassured to find that is so, that adults are at once kind and strong enough to protect them from their own half-wished, half-feared impulses.

Although he may run in and join them in their bed for an early-morning romp sometimes, a child shouldn't be encouraged to sleep with his parents in their bed; parents can make it clear that there are times for the grownups to be alone, although there are occasions when a transitory fear or bad dream call for comforting and even a regression to wanting to be held or carried is understandable.

On such occasions a child can be taken into his parents' bed or joined by one of them in his without changing overall policy. It depends on what his overriding need is at the moment. On the whole, showing him that you protect your own privacy while granting him his will make it easier for him to accept some inevitable limitations.

The passing fears which are so common at this age are often associated with some wish the child feels is unacceptable to the adults who are so important to him or even unacceptable to his own conscience. He is afraid that this forbidden wish—for instance, to have his mother all to himself—will come to the surface and cause him to lose his parents' love and protection, and to keep this from happening he doesn't express his real fear but displaces it onto something else.

The child with a phobia is basically not afraid of school or dogs or elevators but of the loss of his parents' love. The anger he feels toward them makes him afraid and he displaces this fear onto something else. It is a common human phenomenon to transfer feelings in this way. Probably the best way to avoid such phobic reactions is to allow the child to express his hostile thoughts and angry impulses in words and allow him to see that he is not destroyed or abandoned because of them. He needs to learn to accept his angry feelings along with the rest of himself as long as he does not act destructively on them. And the only way for him to learn this is to see that you accept him, "naughtiness" and all—that thoughts do no harm and that even when you disapprove of his actions you do not stop loving him.

Fears and nightmares, wanting to stay close to mother and father, or calling out repeatedly from his bed at night to make sure they are still there are patterns of behavior which often occur following a child's separation from his parents, even when it is a short one, and even though he may not outwardly seem to object to their absence.

A little boy whose mother and father have left him at home and gone on a trip or whose mother has gone to the hospital to have another baby, or whose father has separated from his mother and left home may feel furiously angry at them, although he may not show it, for what he sees as their having abandoned him this way. When the parents return from their vacation or the mother comes home from the hospital or the father comes to visit on a Sunday afternoon the child may have to express the hostility he feels toward them for having left him. If he is afraid to do so, if he is not allowed to put into words or play what he feels inside—if he is made to feel unloved for sulking instead of saying hello, or for bursting into tears of reproach instead of smiles of welcome—he may translate his feelings about these separations into seemingly unrelated fears.

The monsters in the closet, the beasts under the bed, may not be real, but the feeling of fear the child has, whatever its original source, is very real indeed. The most helpful thing parents can do is not to try to analyze or interpret the fears but to be his parents—to give him comfort and affectionate reassurance that they will never really desert him, that they will protect him no matter what. In most cases, that is enough to vanquish beast and monster alike.

15

The School Years: Beginning to Let Go

IN CONSIDERING SOME of the problems that come up in the school years, the years between early childhood and adolescence which we might call "middle childhood," we're going to continue to avoid being very specific about age, because doing so makes it hard for parents to resist trying to elicit a certain response if it does not appear spontaneously at the "normal" age. We want to continue to look at the implications of children's behavior at different levels of development, regardless of the exact age at which they occur. We will continue to "skip around," from infancy to adolescence, from early childhood to young adulthood and back again, to show how the processes of development weave through the growing years and relate to the different stages in a human being's life; how the trust developed in infancy influences the ability to make friends as a child and to love as a grownup; how responsibilities given a two-year-old relate to his adolescent behavior at home and in school.

After all, adult behavior doesn't just emerge in adulthood. It is a complex and interrelated set of patterns formed in response to the earliest life experiences as well as those that come afterward.

With this in mind, let's look at some of the problems that arise in children anywhere from five to eleven who are no longer babies and not yet adolescents—how these problems relate to earlier experiences and how they prefigure later behavior. Here again we are concerned with what the general direction of development at this stage of life should be, so you can keep this in mind in choosing solutions that will be adaptive for *your* child—that will encourage healthy growth and prevent serious emotional illness.

In many ways, the elementary-school years are the most peaceful in a child's life—and the easiest on his parents. By now he is able to do many things for himself. He no longer requires the amount of time or the kind of attention he did when his mother had to mediate between him and the environment. Now in many ways he deals directly with the world of things and people on his own. He dresses himself, goes to school, makes his own arrangements to play with other boys and girls, and begins to get around his neighborhood, his town or city on his own. For the most part, these things come about gradually with none of the tension and turmoil that so often accompanies his development a few short years from now, in adolescence.

The first manifestation of the school child's new independence comes as he begins to separate himself from home and family, spending more of his time in the company of others his own age. It is as though children at this time and during adolescence find emotional support for the journey from home in each other's company. They belong to their own groups, organize clubs and secret societies, and have their own codes and special languages, their own rituals in games, chants and jokes, all of which emphasize their solidarity and separation from adults—

and sometimes from the opposite sex as well. Girls become very involved in personal relationships, making friends and enemies, often of the same people on succeeding days, gossiping and telling secrets. Boys' social life is more rough-and-tumble, and they seem to punch and wrestle as naturally as they walk. Large muscle development at this age seems to require a certain amount of motor activity and it is hard for the child to sit still at the dinner table or in school, where he may seem to do as much wriggling and squirming and doodling as reading and writing. He has a real need for this discharge of energy and teachers often find it more useful to expect it and give the third- or fourth-grade boy a certain leeway to move around as he listens and does his work. Imposing immobility at this age often builds up a level of tension which makes it impossible for the child to concentrate and does more to interfere with academic progress than to foster it.

This is the great age of collections, and boys and girls hoard and trade everything from matchbooks and bottle caps to butterflies and stamps. These collections may represent a kind of symbolic mastery of the environment, giving the child control of the world reduced to objects on a scale where he can manage and order them. They are also a manifestation of the child's capacity to involve himself in the world of other people, serving as a medium of social exchange between a group of boys who, for example, may collect and exchange baseball cards or marbles. As in every phase of childhood, playing is learning, and social and intellectual skills are being mastered in what the child does after school as well as in the classroom. He needs time for fooling around, for what looks like time-wasting. A child who seems to a parent to be doing nothing at all may actually be doing something very important for his personality growth and development. He may be reflecting on the choices open to him in play or

179

social life, or just getting practice in structuring his own time, planning his own activity. This is a time for learning, but not for too much pressure or too much organized activity. He needs a little time for daydreaming, too, and a corner of his own to do it in. The exuberant mother with good intentions who programs every minute may be unknowingly interfering with this very important process.

Part of the experimentation with life at this age involves the child's tendency to try a new thing, a game or perhaps a food, and keep at it relentlessly for a while, then drop it completely and take up something new. Fads are one of the ways he finds out what he likes, which is part of knowing who he is, and it's doubtful whether any child was ever really harmed by playing nothing but Monopoly for a week or eating hamburgers for lunch all through a whole November. He'll get tired of it and go on to something else—and sooner if it's at his own pace, not yours. Wise parents at this stage begin to give the child as much control of his own body as he can cope with. It may be more important for him to feel he can make some decisions for himself than to wear his galoshes or finish his dinner.

Children usually love school if they are not physically restricted or treated with hostility. They need a world of their own, to some extent to replace their family, which was their whole world until now. And if they find it in school, they do not have to look for it on the street or in antisocial gangs. Because they have a tendency to involve themselves in the outside world and are not troubled and distracted with the drives and tensions that will come with adolescence, these years offer a great opportunity for learning. They are receptive to new ideas and people, and are developing new intellectual capacities. However, not until around the age of ten or eleven do most children have the capacity to deal meaningfully with abstractions such as mathematical logic, historical time or causal relationships not related to their own physical experience. A number of studies in recent years have shown that although children may verbalize about such things as temporal relationships or physical causes, they often lack any real understanding of the concepts involved. What children say should not always be taken as a reliable indication of how much they understand. The fact that they are able to memorize dates or formulas is no guarantee that they have any clear idea of how much time elapsed between one historical event and another unless they can relate them to events in their own lives, or that they can understand ideas of mass, weight and density unless they have an opportunity to feel and touch things, pick them up and experience the pull on their own muscles.

The best way to take advantage of school-age children's receptivity to learning is to provide them with enough of the kinds of experiences with which they *can* cope—arithmetic they can master by themselves, history as stories of people, scientific ideas in ways they can see and touch and feel—giving them a feeling of their own competence rather than pushing them beyond what they are developmentally able to cope with mentally and perhaps setting up a negative reaction. Again, as in infancy, too much stimulation leads to withdrawal, but the child who has been exposed to gradually increasing amounts of stimulation all along will have developed both the cognitive capacity and the attitude that enable him to cope with new and increasingly demanding situations.

Occasionally around the middle school years boys and girls become disagreeable and argumentative at home, even though they get along well enough with friends at school. They always seem to be claiming "that's not fair!" Standing up to you verbally may be another way of asserting their independence. The best response is probably the least response. Your child shouldn't feel he can manipulate you into changing your ideas or plans, but while remaining firm you needn't be angry or reject him. It won't be the last time in the course of his growing up that you'll be called upon as parents to be tolerant of his idiosyncrasies in order to help him to find himself, to establish his identity as one who can cope with the outside world on his own.

Sometime during childhood all boys and girls explore their body and find that masturbatory activity gives them pleasure. There is nothing wrong or abnormal about this unless it begins to take the place of other activities and other means of meeting stressful situations. Exploration and self-stimulation are normal phases of sexual development and unless they become substitutes for other things there is really no reason to try to keep the child from doing them in private. If this activity is neither encouraged nor met with horror and a punitive attitude, it will diminish in time. Parents should make it clear that masturbation is not done in front of others and is somewhere in the category of not-exactly-desirable behavior, but should certainly not suggest that it is wicked or harmful. Guilt does more harm than masturbation.

When the world seems mean and cruel a child may occasionally turn to himself for comfort. He may fall back on self-arousal to give himself love when he feels unloved or unwanted. If this becomes his main source of gratification, he loses out on the period when he should be learning to get gratification from various schoolwork tasks and the give-and-take of games and sports and play. The best solution is a positive one—to provide his life with other kinds of gratification, other sources of acceptance, which means love to him at this age. Overreacting explicitly to early masturbatory behavior may tend to make a child feel he can get recognition through exhibiting his body and overemphasize behavior associated with sexual prowess.

It's important that children get their information about reproduction and birth from their parents when they first become curious, before the capacity for sexual arousal colors what they can understand with their feelings and fantasies.

Around the age of three every healthy child is full of questions about everything he sees around him. He is bent on finding out what things are called, what they are for, how they work, where they came from. Young children's interest in sex is no different from their interest in everything about themselves and their world and should be treated by parents in the same way. Questions about the differences between boys and girls, about where babies come from, about *how* the seed gets planted, and where, and what happens after that, should be answered with the same directness, on a level the child can understand, as his questions about what clouds are, how the vegetables get to the supermarket, and what makes the doorbell ring. At this age, sexual information only becomes loaded emotionally if you give what are obviously more elaborately detailed answers than you do in responding to all his other questions, or if you avoid answering his questions or seem tense in doing so. A child whose sexual curiosity is squelched now may show less interest in exploring the world generally. He learns not to ask questions, and a head full of unanswered questions will not prove the easiest one to put arithmetic or history into later on.

In order to orient himself to his peer group, the main task of this period of development, the child must be able to detach himself from his parents and from parental expectations part of the time. He has to comply at school in

183

order to learn, and he has to carry out certain responsibilities at home, but in addition he has to have some leeway for experimenting with new roles for himself and new ways of relating to people outside his home.

If he cannot begin to detach himself emotionally from his parents because he has not acquired the necessary trust in them and confidence in himself earlier in life, he will have difficulty finding the emotional energy to go out to meet the world now. If he is enmeshed in trying to resolve old problems, he hasn't the interest to try new things. He'll be constantly fluctuating between two stages in development and this will slow down his progress in those attempts to find out who he is and what he can do which are so important at this age.

Boys and girls in middle childhood are anxious about the weaknesses they fear they may have themselves and sometimes feel threatened when they see them in others. They sometimes manifest their anxiety in what looks like meanness or seeming indifference to the weakling, the "cry baby" or the misfit in their midst. They have a tendency to identify with the strong and mighty, with kings, supermen and heroes. Little children start out wanting to be policemen or others they perceive as authority figures because they want to take on some of their power—to be able to relieve suffering and thus master the environment as doctors do, to manipulate armies as generals do, to make people cheer as presidents do. They need their heroes, their policemen or generals or presidents, because they need ideals to serve as models of the strengths they hope to acquire, particularly at a time when they have to begin detaching themselves from their own parents. The child who hears about corruption in the police or in government is often devastated and may begin at that point to start thinking seriously about identifying with the robbers, not the cops. The child who perceives authorities not as protective figures but as punitive ones, like the slum child, is also deprived of models of adult behavior to identify with.

These are the years when children begin to establish various social roles. They are engaged in a long-range effort to become part of the outside world, to be accepted by it, and they have to find their way in the world of their peers, the world of school and gangs and clubs and secret organizations that the adult world is excluded from. The child who is kept from this important process by being too involved with grownups and too oriented to their expectations of him may have difficulty finding a mate later on, when he will still be looking for a figure more adult than himself to relate to.

Of course, the school-age child is not ready to move out of the house and away from his family altogether. That comes much later. He still needs much in the way of emotional support, information only they can give him, and opportunities to identify with his parents in time spent together. Home and family should be there for him to turn to when he needs them. But parents should realize that he is beginning to need them a little less all the time, and do nothing to interfere with that natural and healthy process.

The child with a handicap, a chronic disease or physical disability, or even the normal child who receives special attention only when he is sick, often makes illness the basis of his way of relating to other people. Parents have to be careful not to reinforce these directions through their attitudes, not to place a premium on a kind of behavior that can only retard the child's development. Sometimes the attitude toward life is more crippling than the disease or disability itself.

Whatever kind of behavior is rewarded by parental attention will be reinforced in a child. Parents sometimes

185

reinforce failure in the child who plays the clown, who finds it is his misfortunes, not his successes, that bring him attention from others. Some clinicians even feel that many older people who become sickly after retirement although their sickness has no clear organic basis have taken on the illness role because they were brought up to feel that people should work unless they are sick. The only way they can justify to themselves their not working is to relate to other people as if they were ill.

Sometimes parents try to influence a child's life interests, even his eventual choice of a vocation or profession, too strongly and too soon. They may insist on his practicing a musical instrument he hates, going to a kind of camp he doesn't enjoy, push him into competitive games, even throw him off a diving board. These efforts, of course, usually do more to mold dislikes than interests, as many an adult who can't play a note of music, avoids sports or can't swim will testify. Besides, it's probably too early to influence the direction of a child's ultimate career except in the subtlest of ways. And the best way to influence him in anything is by being a parent he will wind up trusting—one he will realize has his long-range interests at heart.

Children with many skills, with talents they pursue to the point of achievement and personal satisfaction, are usually those whose parents watched for signs of interest initiated by the child himself and then responded positively, whether by appreciating his accomplishments, finding him a teacher, buying him materials or helping in some other way. It's even a good idea if the child has to put forth some effort along those lines—say by earning a part of the money his drums or his paints will cost. That's what makes it his own project and not just yours.

Children this age have to try many things before they

learn what they really like to do, and what they're good at. The more they try, and find they are able to perservere at until they reach a certain level of competence, the more capable they are likely to be as adults—in ways that may seem totally unrelated to some of these childhood interests. A boy who can organize, lead and perform in a rock-and-roll group at school won't necessarily grow up to be a professional pop musician. He may be gaining a kind of experience, and a kind of feeling about himself, that will make him a good business executive, hospital administrator or schoolteacher. And the longer he waits to make his final choice of a career the better a choice it's likely to be, because it will be based on more experience doing different things in the world and having contact with more people who do still other things.

In the same way, a young girl who spends hours at ballet practice won't necessarily turn out to be a professional dancer, or a boy who's engrossed in judo become a fighter, but these skills help develop the growing body and the creative capacity in addition to forming the habit of practicing skills until one becomes proficient at them, a habit which is eminently transferable to other areas later in life.

What are some of the things that influence whether the process of separation and individuation from parents goes smoothly or not?

Perhaps the most important thing is that the parents be able to accept, emotionally as well as intellectually, the increasing independence of the child and his capacity to engage in a world outside of their influence. The mother who wants to know everything the child does and be a part of the child's world all the time, who feels left out if she's not included in everything he does or makes or plans, will express anxiety over what she feels to be the "loss" of her child and hostility over his excluding her.

This can take subtle forms, from offering to go along every time he decides to go somewhere with a friend to offering her services in cutting out a little girl's paper dolls, building with blocks or writing a book report. It's one thing to provide help and support when they are asked for, and quite another to make his activities central to your life for your gratification. Then you're not helping him, he is helping you, and at some level you are exchanging roles and asking him to take on the function of being a parent to you, providing you with what you need. He's not really equipped to do that yet and such a demand may set up a real stumbling block to his future development. He does have natural tendencies to want to forge out on his own, and your reluctance to have him do so will arouse in him the latent anxiety which is present in all children at being separated from their parents and exists alongside their tendencies to mature behavior. Both the desire to be independent and the desire to remain dependent are present, and it is a question of which will be strengthened at the expense of the other.

The mother who needs to keep her child dependent on her in order to feel he is still close to her is often one who will say, and even think, Oh, I *want* him to go off on his own, to learn to manage for himself, to marry someday and have a family of his own. But in effect she is getting across another and different message, constantly asking, "What did you do in school today?" "Who was that boy I saw you with?" "What do you mean you don't know his name? I've told you you should always find out people's names." "Where are you going now?" "Are you sure you don't want me to help you with that?" She is trying to keep herself involved in the child's world.

All of us would like in some sense to keep our children close beside us, to enjoy their growth as extensions of ourselves beyond our own lives. None of us likes to be rejected or to feel excluded. A shadow of a wish crosses every parent's mind to have a totally loving baby clinging to us forever, not turning into this gangling stranger with the missing teeth and dirty ears who has secrets of his own and would rather go for a bike ride with another boy his own age than stay home and talk with us. But we're the grownups and it is we who have to accept the inevitable, to learn to find gratification in the success of his efforts to do things for himself instead of in doing them for him.

If it is not interfered with, children of school age have a tendency to want to be with their friends, to explore the world and find out who they are. If parents begin to create a sense of guilt in the child about his efforts to leave them for gradually increasing amounts of time and go out into the world on their own, if they constantly hover, question and express disapproval, the child may begin to fear his parents will abandon him—and not loving him means abandonment to a child—if he continues to behave in ways which are unacceptable to them. These are the children who become the sissies, the teacher's pets, the adult-oriented children who behave in ways grownups invariably approve of but who have difficulty relating to other children their own age. They are not really well behaved, just as the baby who does not cry is not really a "good" baby. They too have turned off a kind of responsiveness on which their future healthy development in part depends.

Just as the infant has to continue to reach out to adults in order to learn and grow, the older child has to learn to give and take in relationships with his peers in order to take his place in the adult world eventually. He cannot do so if all of his important relationships continue to be with adults and all his social gratification comes from them, as

189

a result of his fears of abandonment by those on whom he is still emotionally dependent.

Most clinicians who treat school phobias know that parental attitudes are the crucial thing in the development of a fear of being in school as well as in its treatment.

Sometimes poor relations between parents interfere with a child's ability to leave home emotionally. When a mother or father's greatest satisfactions in life come from a child's responses to them rather than from the other parent, the child may develop a clinging attitude in order to comply with the parent's wishes, entering into a mutually dependent relationship based on a sense of his mother's or father's need for him, just at a time when he should be learning to be independent. The mother who is completely involved in everything the child does, who organizes, plans and programs his entire life because of the gratification she gets out of it, may not really be doing the child good. What the child needs is support in getting underway the things *he* is motivated to do.

Parents whose aim is to give their children everything they can, everything they themselves ever wished for, may not be giving them what they need. Sometimes, not parental neglect but parental mismanagement in the guise of the very best intentions interferes with a child's development.

Children have a right to privacy and to some secrets. Don't expect them to tell you their every thought or wish, any more than you would want to tell them yours. Some parents, and some nursery-school teachers, are always asking about a child's fears and dreams. It's one thing to respond to what a child wants to tell you, and quite another to play psychologist. It takes years of training and clinical experience to learn to deal effectively with the unseen roots of behavior; amateurs can't expect to accomplish much without a great deal of understanding of the techniques and goals of psychotherapy. What your child needs from you is mothering or fathering—not psychologizing.

16

Adolescence:
Finding a Place in the World

THE INFANT FOR WHOM the world is a stimulating and gratifying place responds, as soon as he is able to move around on his own, with an eagerness to investigate his world and relate to others in it. When he has gained a sense of self-mastery, balanced by an acceptance of some of the limitations of reality, he is ready to settle down and learn in earnest about the world.

During the school years he forms relationships with others his own age outside the family and masters the new skills of reading, writing and arithmetic. His growth proceeds more or less peacefully, with little of the dramatic change that characterized early infancy or the internal and external struggles that were a part of learning to accept restraints on many of his infantile impulses.

Then, with the approach of puberty, come the first rumblings of a volcano that seems to erupt on the peaceful scene of childhood. We call it adolescence.

Suddenly the nice little girl who used to live in your house doesn't wash her feet, spends hours putting pimple creams on her face, eats only graham crackers one day, four hamburgers at a time the next, and nothing at all the next. She talks to her best friend on the phone for an hour and a half on Monday, baring her inmost secrets, and declares her a dirty rat on Tuesday, adding her intention never to speak to her again. She states categorically that you are incapable of understanding any of her feelings, obviously never having had any of your own that were even faintly similar, and is given to frequent bursts of tears punctuated by the sounds of running feet, slamming doors, and long hours spent alone in what secret rites you dare not even imagine. She seems to be attending a series of costume parties, and you never know whether she will emerge from her room dressed as Mata Hari, a flower child or the girl next door. You only know that it's a sure bet she has either failed to clean her room at all, leaving underwear, science notes and cookie crumbs everywhere, or that she has had a burst of energy and orderliness in which she has thrown out all the little mementos of her childhood that you treasured so and assumed she would keep for *her* daughter.

Many a parent thinks, at this point, that something is seriously wrong. Before calling for professional help, a few observations on adolescence may help.

Adolescence is a period of the most rapid growth and greatest changes in the human being's life except for his first year. This sudden spurt of growth, the changes in his appearance when secondary sexual characteristics like body hair begin to appear at the onset of puberty, the beginning of menstruation in girls, the strange new feelings of arousal that accompany the development of the reproductive system, can be upsetting and, if a youngster has not been prepared for them, even frightening. Not only physical growth but some degree of emotional turmoil is an inevitable part of adolescence.

In all times and every place, the struggle to emerge

from childhood begins by freeing oneself from one's parents. A society like ours intensifies the conflicts involved in the transition from childhood to adulthood because the adolescent matures biologically long before he can take a meaningful place in the grownup world. Girls become women long before they usually become wives, and boys are men before they are considered ready to do a man's work.

In our increasingly complex urban world, physical maturity comes long before the school years are over, and in our increasingly permissive society, the adolescent is exposed to many kinds of stimulation at a time when he is capable of responding to it physically but discouraged from doing so socially. Unless he is able to channel his new energies into other activities such as sports and schoolwork, he will have a tendency to act them out in antisocial ways or withdraw into fantasy. He needs a great deal of gratifying activity, release for motor energy as well as challenges to occupy his mind, but he needs to feel what he is doing is *his* thing, not his parents' idea.

It has been said that abnormality is the normal condition of adolescence. What this means is that behavior which would seem a clear indication of mental imbalance in a person much younger or much older is a routine phenomenon around the age of puberty and for some time thereafter. It doesn't necessarily reflect serious or lasting emotional disorders in a youngster whose early experiences have been well adapted to his developmental needs.

Ponder the difficult position of the poor adolescent—no longer a child, not yet a grownup, and beset by a series of physiological changes unparalleled in their rate by any other time of human growth except infancy. It must be a little like Alice in Wonderland, eating bites without knowing whether she will find herself getting bigger or smaller, and unable to do anything about it anyway. In addition to the many changes in the appearance of one's face and body there are all those new feelings, great surges of energy and emotion one doesn't know how to fulfill or what to do about.

If being a teenager is hard, being the parent of one can be harrowing. A hostile stranger often seems to have taken the place of your loving child, and wherever he came from, he makes no bones about his contempt for your basic life values as well as what you served for dinner last night.

The adolescent's conflict with his parents is not only inevitable—it can be useful too. The adolescent feels he is struggling for his own individuality, and this conflict can provide an opportunity for developing the independence and the skills he'll need for adapting to the kinds of situations he'll face in adult life.

There has to be some conflict between the generations for the young person to take his own turn as an adult. The adolescent whose mother dresses like a teenager and whose father does the craziest new dances will have a pretty hard time of it. "Your parents shouldn't be too much like you," as one teenager put it, sensing that parents should in one sense represent something to move away from. They are like the teenager's radar screen, a device he bounces beams off to see where he's at, a frame of reference against which he tests his position as he tries to find out who he is, and who and what he's up against.

Having something to struggle against helps young people in this difficult position to structure themselves. You are at least on the way to a definition when you know what something is *not*.

"Enlightened" parents are perplexed by the struggle of adolescence, afraid of damaging their children, and sometimes give them too much freedom at this point, hoping to avoid conflict. What they are doing is failing to give their youngsters any certainty or structure to struggle against.

When the teenager in such a family asks what to do about something ("Do you like this skirt?" "Can I go bowling?" "Is this too much lipstick?") her mother may feel, Why should I bother saying anything—she'll only do what she wants anyway. But even if she'll do it her own way and not her mother's, the teenager still needs to know what her mother thinks. Otherwise she has no way of knowing whether she's doing it her way or her mother's! She needs to feel she's finding her own way of doing things. "How," observed one teenager in a wry moment of self-understanding, "can I do the opposite of what you want unless I know what you want?"

The adolescent is involved in a process similar to the individuation that takes place in the infant, but in a different context. Again he has to learn to separate himself from his parents, to perceive his self. Observers sometimes note with amusement that in their struggle to be "different," all teenagers wind up looking just like all the other members of their group. But the point is that while they may look just like all the other kids, they do look different from their parents. And their parents shouldn't try to imitate them.

Their concern with what they look like is typical of adolescents. It makes it easier to accept their constant change of costumes and of masks if one realizes that in a sense they are about to go onstage in a drama—adult life —in which they don't yet know what role they'll play.

There are various options open to the teenager. One response to the challenge of adolescence is clinging to a childish, passive, dependent role as a means of avoiding the responsibilities of adulthood. For instance, a girl may

197

try to remain sexually unattractive by showing no interest in clothes or make-up.

Most teenagers learn to master increased independence and practice the kinds of tasks and responsibilities that go with being a grownup while still living at home. When things don't work out in the big outside world, the adolescent can always run home and find someone there to comfort him.

As at every stage of life, the parent's role should be not to push and not to overprotect them from reality, but to try to help them master reality, to encourage them to use their own resources to cope with the stresses and strains of adult life.

In order to be able to communicate with teenagers—especially one's own—it helps to take into account that exaggeration is an almost universal characteristic of adolescence. The adolescent talks about a new pair of shoes as though the world will come to an end if he does not get them, and punctuates accounts of the most ordinary daily incidents with expressions like "I thought I'd die!" and "I felt like killing him!" His speech reflects strong feelings and may parallel the intensification of drives which he is experiencing physiologically, the enormous physical energy which has to go somewhere.

This is a stage of life at which discomfort and intensity are adaptive. They serve a useful purpose by bringing the adolescent into conflict with people, tasks, situations, so he has an opportunity to master these things. Adolescents need assistance in coping with these feelings, which even frighten themselves sometimes by their intensity. "I know you feel very strongly about this, but I'm sure you'll be able to handle it . . ." is a much more helpful response from a parent than, "You shouldn't really feel so strongly about this" or "You'll get over it." The adolescent *can't* not feel so strongly even if he wants to, and the last thing in the world he wants to be told is that he'll continue changing, even though it's true. He's experiencing enough flux as it is, and having his hands full enough, without constantly being told that what he does feel now he won't feel forever.

Like the infant, the adolescent needs to be able to trust his environment. Parents should try not to be like the doctor who says, "Now this won't hurt at all," and then gives the child a shot. That can only work once. It's better now too to say, "This is going to hurt some, and you can cry if you want to." Then the youngster can mobilize himself against the stress and try to do something about it when it comes. He may either take great pride in not crying or relieve his feelings by doing so. Either one is all right. But if you told him it wouldn't hurt, he feels he's failed when he finds that it really does, and cries.

In the same way, the adolescent needs to know that you recognize his pain—the inevitable difficulties that exist for him at this stage of life—just as he needs to know you'll still continue to maintain your own positions about things no matter how he fluctuates in the process of finding his own way.

We are always told we must love our mother and father, but no one can realistically be expected to have no feelings except loving ones for his parents throughout the process of growing up and separating himself from them.

One way some children deal with hostility to a parent is by making up another one and thinking about him or her instead. Sometimes adolescents relate not to their own parents but to some image of fantasied parents—the ones they wish they had. A boy describes the wonderful cakes his mother bakes—and she turns out to be a high-powered career woman who never sets foot in her kitchen; a girl pretends the gentle all-forgiving heroine of her favorite novel is really her mother in place of the over-critical matron who seems to pick on her night and day. In their fantasies, both of them are making up for what they feel are their parents' shortcomings.

All real parents—like all real children—have short-comings. Only unreal ones do not. A dead parent can be idealized by a young person, even to the point where a girl never marries because she can't ever find anyone to match her absent father in his qualities of perfection. It is hard to detach yourself from an idealized perfect person.

If children are free to feel anything, so long as they do not act out their hostile or aggressive feelings, they have a better chance of learning to handle their feelings in some practical way than if they try to hide them and deny their existence. Parents who are secure about themselves and have some understanding of the process by which children become grownups can afford to accept a certain amount of resentment and hostility from their children during adolescence, knowing that it's only transitory and that the first stage in the child's learning to deal with his feelings is to acknowledge their existence.

You needn't feel overwhelmed or as though you've failed as a parent because your fifteen-year-old scorns hearth and home, seeming to prefer the company of any-one in the world to that of his own family. Like being an adolescent, being the parent of an adolescent can be hard, but the best advice for parents is what we so often tell the youngsters: "Be yourself."

The best principle you can follow is probably to be firm about where you stand on things and at the same time warm and comforting. In this way you meet the young person's needs for both protection and limits. This is the kind of parent a child can relate to, even while struggling to find himself, and does not have to reject totally.

The best basis for dealing with a stranger is probably honesty. He needs to know your real thoughts and feelings and he needs to be able to tell you his, even though they will be different. He is beginning to see things out of his own eyes, not his parents'.

If you tell a child the truth about the consequences of his actions, chances are he'll continue to listen to you as he grows up. Experience has taught him to trust you. But don't expect him to believe you when he's fifteen and you tell him about the dangers of taking LSD if you've lied to him or grossly exaggerated dangers when he was younger.

Both the punitive and the overprotective parent fail to help the child learn to cope with his own feelings in ways that are appropriate to his capacities at each stage of development. That is one reason why so many young people in these circumstances resort to finding some ideal parent figure they feel they can relate to. The many cases of adolescent hero-worship attest to the commonness of this solution. In recent times we've seen another widespread response on the part of the young. If young people have been deprived of parents they feel they can respect, even though they may love them, they may turn to their own peers instead of to adults for standards of conduct and in order to establish their identity and values. This is what the hippies seem to be doing. Overly permissive parents, like overly punitive ones, rob their children of authority figures they can either identify with or rebel against—and both are genuine needs of the growing person. A loving parent can tolerate the rebelliousness when he feels his basically good relationship with his child will reassert itself eventually in the process of identification as he gets older. This is the meaning of the old saw about the son who, at twenty, found his father such an idiot but was amazed to find, when he was thirty, how much his father seemed to have learned.

The related processes that are at work in infants and in teenagers require a certain flexibility on the part of parents. You have to change, to be a "different parent" at different stages of the child's development, indulgent when he is powerless to do things for himself, firm when he needs to learn just how far he can go by himself, and stable and comforting when he needs to alternate between trying his own wings and returning to the nest.

If you try to keep the larger developmental goals of each stage of growth in mind instead of just responding in terms of what will gratify the child or yourself at the moment, chances are your day-to-day dealings with him will result in a basically healthy child—one who will be able to deal effectively with the present as he grows up.

Many life decisions, such as the choice of occupation and of a husband or wife, are influenced by the way one resolves the conflicts of the various earlier stages of development. All of us have neurotic drives we channel in some particular ways that are socially acceptable and help us adjust to reality. We all have unacceptable impulses at various moments in our lives. Some people never learn to deal with them in socially acceptable ways and may even become criminals. Others learn to channel them in ways that are useful to society and help them live gratifying lives.

The basis for many occupational choices is some childhood impulse mastered and channeled into the individual's life plan. A child who likes to witness pain or a child who is terrified of being hurt may be led to become a surgeon or a nurse long after the childish hostility or fear is forgotten—just as a curious or nosy child may become a psychologist or a writer and wind up getting paid for finding out about other people's lives.

And whether a young woman marries a man who is just like her father or as unlike him as possible, she is still responding to the present in terms of the past. To the extent to which she is unaware of the factors in her decision which do not belong to the present, she is liable to make the wrong choices for her future. It's a kind of mental health insurance, therefore, to help young people be aware of and learn to deal with as many of their conflicting feelings as possible. The world is full of grownups whose own parents may not even still be alive but who are operating in such a way, without even realizing it, as to win their parents' approval.

The young have always been impatient, discontented with the world of the old and anxious to change it. Young activists seem to be characterized by a degree of skepticism along with their passion for reform. We don't always know whether their protest leads to real changes. But discomfort—"maladjustment"—is not always a sign of sickness or weakness. The important thing is to help young people not to be overwhelmed by their dissatisfaction with the way things are, not to respond either by just giving up or by aimless destructive behavior, but to try to cope with reality in such a way as to bring about change for the better, in themselves and in their environment.

For many people, frustration seems to result from a sense of inability to change their environment. The feeling that they are powerless to change things they are dissatisfied with detracts from a sense of purpose in their lives and creates a void they sometimes attempt to fill with any act—however destructive—that will seem to leave their mark on things. (Another reason for becoming a psychologist or a writer—you can feel you help bring about changes in people and in the world!)

Increasing numbers of young women seem reluctant to stay home and do something they feel anyone else can do just as well. (They may apply to housework but definitely not—as we hope this book shows—to child care!) Once the basic necessities of life are provided for, people begin to look around for ways to realize themselves. We all seem to need to ask at some point, "Will it make any difference that I've been here?"

Even babies and young children need to feel they can affect the world around them. Clinicians see this need dramatically manifested in the plight of sick youngsters. The child in the hospital feels powerless to manipulate his environment. He has to lie still while he is examined. He has to stay where he doesn't want to be. He has to do without the most important people in his life for long hours at a time. He has to submit to unpleasant and often painful procedures. The job of the people taking care of him is to help him feel he is not entirely lost, not without any will of his own. Even little things can help. A nurse may ask, "Would you like a red or a green lollipop after the examination?" This is even better than, "If you're a good boy you can have a lollipop afterward." He has to undergo the examination, but he is also being given some opportunity, however small, to express himself, to make a choice, to participate in his own fate.

In a similar way, even healthy children, especially at critical points in their development, benefit from the knowledge that what happens to them, at home and at school, is influenced by what they do, how they behave.

One of the most important things we can try to do for our children is help them to meet adulthood equipped to deal with the world as it really is and make real changes in it, rather than dissipate their energies in fantasies or withdrawal from responsibility.

THE BEST OF BESTSELLERS
FROM WARNER BOOKS!

A STRANGER IN THE MIRROR by Sidney Sheldon **(89-204, $1.95)**
This is the story of Toby Temple, superstar and super bastard, adored by his vast TV and movie public, but isolated from real human contact by his own suspicion and distrust. It is also the story of Jill Castle, who came to Hollywood to be a star and discovered she had to buy her way with her body. When these two married, their love was so strong it was—**terrifying!**

THE SUMMER DAY IS DONE by R.T. Stevens **(89-270, $1.95)**
In the tradition of **Love's Tender Fury** and **Liliane** comes **The Summer Day Is Done,** the haunting story of a forbidden love between the secret agent of the King of England and the daughter of the Imperial Czar.

THE STAR SPANGLED CONTRACT **(89-259, $1.95)**
by Jim Garrison
From the first crack of the rifle, former undercover agent Colin McFerrin is flung headlong into a maze of deception and death as he tries desperately to save the President from assassins within his own government. "A chilling book . . . a knowledgeable, suspenseful thriller . . . first-rate, charged with menace. It will keep you glued to the printed page."—**John Barkham Reviews**

LORETTA LYNN: COAL MINER'S DAUGHTER **(89-252, $1.95)**
by Loretta Lynn with George Vecsey
It's a Horatio Alger story with a country beat, "so open, honest and warm that it's irresistible."—**New York News.** 100,000 copies sold in hardcover!

 A Warner Communications Company

Please send me the books I have checked.

Enclose check or money order only, no cash please. Plus 35¢ per copy to cover postage and handling. N.Y. State residents add applicable sales tax.

Please allow 2 weeks for delivery.

WARNER BOOKS
P.O. Box 690
New York, N.Y. 10019

Name ....

Address ....

City .... State .... Zip ....

_____ Please send me your free mail order catalog

THE BEST OF BESTSELLERS
FROM WARNER BOOKS!